For our rational
Revolutionary.
Peter + SuzAnne

INSIDE
THE
BLACK
ROOM

INSIDE THE BLACK ROOM

JACK A.
VERNON
Ph. D.

Clarkson N. Potter, Inc./Publisher
New York

 Library of Congress Catalog Card Number: 62-19288. Printed in the United States of America.

To three fine people:

B. J. V.

S.M.V.

V.L.V.

TABLE OF CONTENTS

ACKNOWLEDGMENT

In an acknowledgment it is difficult to do justice to all the people who make a book possible. I cannot spell out and give adequate credit for all the planning and anxiety and just plain hard labor that went into a research project of this nature. I have been very fortunate in having excellent graduate student assistants, and it seems to me a very inadequate acknowledgment only to mention their names. It is my hope that they understand that I feel a great debt of gratitude to them. What value there is in this book I attribute to them, while I alone am responsible for its faults.

Those who have served as research assistants are: Dr. Thomas E. McGill, Dr. Walter L. Gulick, Dr. Douglas Candland, Dr. Harold Shiffman, Dr. Ronald Cromly-Dillon, Dr. Theodore Marton, Dr. Ernest Peterson, Dr. Peter Suedfeld and Dr. Robert Grissom.

The entire project was made possible by a generous grant-in-aid of research given by the Office of the Surgeon General of the Army, and by the National Science Foundation; these agencies provided the ideal atmosphere for research by allowing me complete freedom to conduct the work as I saw fit.

INTRODUCTION

THE study of sensory deprivation involves the restriction of a man alone in a small cubicle where he can perceive neither light nor sound. In talking about such experiments to people, in general I have encountered an almost standard set of reactions. The first reaction, and probably my major reason for venturing this book, is that of keen interest. Most people are swept up in the uniqueness of the situation and are fascinated by the findings.

A second, and very common, reaction is to ask about any possible application of these findings. Most people assume that we have set out to solve some specific problem or have attempted to find some specific application. I always answer by saying that no particular use of what we learned is or was planned. We set out merely in the hope of gaining a bit of new knowledge about man, and in particular about man under some rather unusual conditions. Indeed, we realize that we have now perhaps done little more than define some problems about human conduct which will be carried forward by other investigators.

I have stated that our work was not aimed at any

particular application. However, it has been impossible for most people not to speculate a bit about two likely and obvious uses. The conditions of the confinement used in our work resemble certain parts of the "indoctrination" procedures as practiced by the Red Chinese in the Korean War. One of their purposes was to reeducate the United Nations prisoners to their political beliefs. The process they utilized, termed "brainwashing," was a complicated affair and is not our concern here, except that it was often started by placing the prisoner in solitary confinement. Our work in sensory deprivation (henceforth "S.D.") involved, among other things, solitary confinement. Both brainwashing and S.D. will be considered in more detail later.

Another application of our work has been suggested in its possible relation to space flight. This application is not nearly so relevant, for, it seems to me, the conditions of space flight are greatly different from those of S.D.: space flight does not deprive a man of sight and sound the way S.D. does; also, space flight must be a very exciting affair, unlike the extreme boredom of S.D. Nevertheless there is a similarity between the two, as space flight involves a form of isolation as well as restriction to a confined area.

I should point out, however, that a program of studies in sensory deprivation has been initiated by the Aerospace Medical Laboratory at Wright-Patterson Air Force Base, Ohio. The original effort was headed by the research team of George Ruff, Edwin Levy, and

Victor Thaler, who were interested in the reduction of variability and quantity of sensory stimulation as a potential hazard to space flight.

I hasten to add here that it is primarily others who have applied the S.D. data to brainwashing and space flight, and that to do so is to engage in little more than guessing. When more accurate knowledge is desired about brainwashing or space medicine, it will be found by more direct research.

The reader should understand that, while our goal is pure knowledge for its own sake, we have no objection to someone's use of that knowledge. Though in the past this has happened many times, in many other areas of investigation, the reader should also understand that ultimate application of the data is in no way necessary for our satisfaction. Our only hope was, and still is, to discover a little bit more about man.

People frequently ask how these studies began. Oddly enough, their origin lay in the attempt to solve a specific problem. It seems that radar observers, radio monitors, truck drivers, and others who have very monotonous and routine jobs that last for long periods are often subject to unusual sensory effects. They see a radar pip that isn't there, they hear messages that aren't real, they see hitchhikers who don't exist, or they experience a wide variety of other bizarre sensory distortions. These matters came to the attention of the Canadian Defense Research Board, which asked Dr.

D. O. Hebb, a psychologist at McGill University, to look into the problem. Dr. Hebb, working with such men as Drs. Woodrow Heron, T. H. Scott, W. H. Bexton, and B. K. Doane, began the type of research we have followed.

The reasons I've given above for the origin of the McGill University work, while true, are not the whole story. Though the researchers were not permitted to say so in their first publications, the main reason for their work was the problem of brainwashing. The interested reader can find a more complete account of this in Chapter II of the book *Sensory Deprivation*, edited by Philip Solomon and others, and published in 1961 by Harvard University Press.

There are many questions that will force themselves upon the reader as he becomes familiar with S.D. work. For example, when sensory stimulation has been so drastically reduced, will the mind become obsessed with its need, as does the starving man, whose every thought is of food? Could the S.D. subject be content with an occasional spot of light where he had previously wanted high-talent TV shows? Would a simple sound offer as much pleasure as he previously derived from hi-fi? Do our jaded senses gain a new appreciation for stimulation as a result of practically losing it? And what about social isolation? Does the man in S.D. come to appreciate fellow man more, or does he come to view the experimenters as his captors? If the latter is the case, does he view the one who releases him as his savior? These and many more are still unanswered questions, and therein lies part of the fascination of S.D. work. It tends to generate interesting questions about the most interesting of all things in nature—man.

Since the work at McGill University, many other investigators have worked on specific aspects of sensory deprivation. The work of others will be presented with ours where it is relevant.

I became involved in S.D. because of a student named John Hoffman, who majored in psychology. At Princeton each senior must conduct a piece of research called the senior thesis, as part of the graduation requirement. Usually he has a faculty adviser to whom he sounds out his plans and with whom he works. John came to me at the beginning of his senior year with the suggestion that he work on the "black box" phenomenon for his thesis.

The term "black box" was at that time a popular but totally incorrect reference to the work done at McGill University by Dr. Hebb and his associates. John Hoffman's plan to conduct similar studies attracted me. What he started in 1954 is still active, for, as with most research, the findings have served to stimulate more research.

INSIDE THE BLACK ROOM

PART ONE

How and Why S.D.?

CHAPTER I

What is S.D.?

SENSORY deprivation, or S.D., is a term used to describe the conditions of our experiments, and it is probably not a very good one, since it is inaccurate, but a more precise term becomes wordy and clumsy. Let me explain. The word "sensory" applies to the sense faculties of man—seeing, hearing, smelling, tasting, feeling. And the term "deprivation" means to "take entirely away." Now obviously we did not, and could not, take *entirely* away the action of all the senses. It is possible to deprive the visual sense totally by extinguishing light, but it is not possible to do a similar thing with hearing. Even if a man is placed in a completely soundproof chamber, where no external sounds will reach him, he will still experience auditory sensations. He will hear blood coursing through those blood vessels that are near the ear. He will hear his breathing movements as well as occasional rumblings of the stomach, and the like. It is easily possible to prevent sensations of odor and taste by merely removing stimuli, but man must eat, and food, of course, serves to stimulate both of these senses. In addition to these, the mind also receives sensory stimulation that informs it of body movements, body positions, movements of muscles, changes in temperature, feelings of thirst and hunger, etc. Thus it can be easily appreciated that to deprive man totally of sensory stimulation would be a very difficult, if not impossible, task. There are many who claim that if a person were so deprived his brain would cease functioning. This altogether reasonable belief holds that sensory stimulation, in addition to having its normal function of bringing information to the individual, serves to keep the brain active, alert, and alive.

Almost every investigator has used a different set of conditions for S.D. work, so it is necessary to state them in order to compare the various findings. At this point the conditions employed by Dr. Hebb and our own will be described. Later, when other investigators are introduced, their conditions will be noted.

The workers at McGill confined adult males, one at a time, to a small *lighted* semisoundproof cubicle. Each subject was asked to stay as long as possible, which usually turned out to be two or three days. During confinement the subject wore a semitranslucent goggle that admitted diffuse light but prevented patterned vision. Hearing was restricted by the masking afforded by the sound of an air-conditioner. It is primarily with vision and hearing that the conditions in our work vary from those of the McGill studies.

At Princeton we attempted to provide what we considered as the next phase—drastic reductions in sensory stimulation. We placed our subjects in a lightproof and soundproof room. Within this room was a cubicle that measured four feet in width, nine feet in length, eight feet in height, its floor space practically filled by a king-size bed. The subject was asked to remain on the bed except when obtaining food or using the toilet. Food was provided in the form of sandwiches, fresh fruit, and soup placed in a picnic icebox at the foot of the bed. Toilet facilities were provided by a chemical receptacle placed inside the soundproof room but outside the confinement cubicle, and additionally by relief bottles placed inside the chamber.

The soundproof room is one that was specially constructed in the basement of Princeton's Eno Hall (which, incidentally, though it was built as recently as 1924, is believed to be the first building in the world devoted exclusively to psychology). Soundproofing was achieved by building a "floating room" arrangement—a room within a room. The outer room is a shell of sixteen-inch reinforced concrete. The inner room has eight-inch walls that are separated by a five-inch air gap from the outer room. The floor of the inner room is separated from the outer room much in the fashion of a dry moat. The floor of the inner room is eight inches of concrete that rests on five inches of sand contained in a five-inch concrete saucer, resting in turn on five inches of sand contained by another concrete saucer, which stands upon eighteen inches of crushed rock. Such construction was necessary to prevent sound vibrations from traveling through the ground and entering the room. The walls and ceiling of the floating rooms are lined with soft fiberboard, which partially absorbed noises made within the cubicle. In this regard each subject was instructed to lie as quietly as was comfortably possible and not to make *any* noise such as talking aloud, humming, singing, and the like. A concealed microphone, by which the experimenters frequently "listened in," revealed that our subjects obeyed these instructions almost to a man. The monitoring also found most subjects obeying the command not to move about the cubicle but to remain on the bed.

To these conditions we added absolute lightproofing; that is, there was no illumination inside the room, nor was any lighting possible. There were no light leaks and no facilities for making light once the door was closed. The soundproofing was not absolute, but was about as nearly so as possible. We could have achieved further sound absorption within the cubicle if an anechoic (producing no echoes) chamber had been used, but such a room is quite elaborate and too expensive to warrant the additional gains. As it was, the chamber offered an eighty-decible sound loss, which is considerable soundproofing. The decibel (db) is the unit of measure for sound intensity. A pneumatic hammer makes about eighty db of noise, a boiler shop makes about a hundred db of noise, while airplane engines make about a hundred ten db. Thus it can be seen that our cubicle was adequate for shutting out almost all sounds.

THOSE WHO SERVED AS SUBJECTS

About a hundred subjects have been utilized in our S.D. studies to date. All of these came to us of their own free will. For their services each subject was paid twenty dollars per confinement day or any partial day, and those who served as control subjects were paid five dollars for the two hours or so of tests. A control subject is one who takes the same tests as the confinement subject, but without going into S.D., and thereby forms a comparison to those who do.

Almost all of our subjects were graduate students in the various departments of Princeton. This means that our subjects were alike in that they all were male, of high intelligence, and were between the ages of twenty and thirty-two. They were different in that they came from widely different backgrounds and from different nationalities.

We have strongly wanted a group of less intelligent subjects for additional studies, but so far we have continued to work with the subjects who are most available. Two investigators, Drs. Goldberg and Holt, working at the Research Center for Mental Health at New York University and using conditions somewhat similar to those of the McGill studies, reported in a newspaper article that people of high intelligence tolerate S.D. less well than those of lower intelligence. Other phases of their work are available in the book *Sensory Deprivation*, edited by Philip Solomon and others, already mentioned. There can be no doubt that studies of S.D. using females, or old people, or very young subjects would provide interesting information, but this is research that remains to be done.

For most of our studies we used people who knew very little about S.D. However, the days of having such naïve subjects are just about over, owing to the considerable publicity that has now been given to work in this field.

Our subjects heard about the S.D. experiments pretty much by word of mouth. We usually asked each to mention our need for volunteers to his friends. Because this plan worked so well we had to caution each subject *not* to reveal anything about the experiment to anyone else for fear of influencing the findings from some potential subject, and this also worked very well.

It is generally true that most people who serve in psychological experiments demonstrate a strong tendency to produce what they think are the desired data. Thus in many cases and especially in some of the S.D. studies it has been essential that the subjects not know what data were desired. We have not explained the data to the subjects and we have admonished them not to discuss their experiences in S.D. We feel that for the most part our subjects have not known what to expect.

The immediate reaction of many people upon learning of the conditions of S.D. was to claim that they could not last more than several hours, if at all, in such a situation. Since no one could really know in advance how he would react to S.D., we provided a means of "escape" even after he had committed himself to the study. In the confinement cubicle and easily within his reach we provided a "panic button." Each subject was instructed that if he pushed that button it would summon the experimenter, who would release him from S.D. To push the button for any reason whatsoever would terminate his stay in S.D., that is, he could not push the button merely to bring the experimenter into the room, and then be allowed to continue the experiment.

To describe the "panic button" to the subject was a rather delicate affair. In the first place, we wanted him to understand that S.D. was not a study of stress or an attempt to, in any way, break him down; and we wanted him to know that he could get out if he felt he needed to. At the same time, we did not want to emphasize the necessity for a panic button or that S.D. was such an ordeal that he could expect to panic. We adopted the procedure of telling the truth—that some people found S.D. worse than expected, that they desired release from it, and that the button was provided for such a contingency. Up to the present we have found that about one out of five subjects uses the release button, but, interestingly enough, we cannot predict in advance who they will be.

In the room adjoining the S.D. chamber an experimenter was present throughout the confinement. The constant presence of the experimenter was for safety and testing as well as for availability to heed the panic button should it be used. The subjects knew that an experimenter was always on hand, and many indicated that knowledge of his presence provided a source of comfort to them. Most subjects also indicated that as S.D. wore on they came to believe that the experimenter had deserted them, but such was never the case, for we had made it one of our first rules that no subject would be left unmonitored. I now believe that some of our data would have been very different if we had. It appears that the effects of true social isolation can be appreciated only if the confined subject believes that he is left entirely on his own.

In summary, then: We attempted to determine how man would react to very novel conditions where he is almost entirely dependent upon his own resources. The various studies we conducted involved confinement for from twenty-four hours to ninety-six hours. Some subjects indicated that they could have stayed longer; some demanded release long before twenty-four hours.

CHAPTER II

What It was Like

AT THE termination of each subject's session in S.D. he was given the microphone of a tape recorder and asked to tell what S.D. had been like. We had a standardized set of questions which were informally interjected where appropriate. By and large, however, the subject was unconstrained and free to report as he wished. Some few subjects needed a bit of prodding because they tended to forget their experiences. They may have repressed certain items, but that doesn't seem likely, for they spoke quite freely when reminded.

The beginning of S.D. was viewed in the same way by practically all subjects. Their thoughts are best expressed by the statement of one of the subjects when he said, "I entered the cell that was to become the deepest darkness I have ever known." Many of the subjects even felt that the confinement cubicle was darker than the antechamber where the chemical toilet was located. Both areas were actually equally dark. The darkness of the cubicle may hold significance for the next thing that happened.

Soon after entering the confinement cell most subjects went to sleep and slept almost uninterruptedly for ten to twenty-four hours. These are gross estimates, for there was nothing by which the subjects could determine elapsed time, and if anything they probably *under*estimated sleeping time. We know for certain that one subject slept for nineteen hours but insisted that he had had a nap of less than one hour. According to the monitoring microphone, which was capable of picking up the deep breathing of sleep, it seems more likely that most subjects slept almost all of the first twenty-four hours.

We felt that so much sleeping in the first day wasted the effects of confinement, so we started placing subjects in S.D. early in morning. We reasoned that after a night's sleep our confined subject would be unable to dissipate the effects of S.D. by sleeping. Such was not the case. As far as we could determine they went to sleep just as quickly and slept just as long as the previous subjects. We then started entering the subjects at midmorning, midday, and midafternoon. As it turned out, it made no difference when during the day and, presumably, during the night we started the confinement; the initial sleep period was always about the same.

We had not expected this extended period of initial sleep. In fact, it had seemed reasonable to expect something of the opposite. S.D. was a very novel situation for our subjects, and as such, we reasoned, it should have occupied him for some time. I had a similar expectation for astronauts during space flight and was greatly surprised to learn that the Russian astronaut Yuri Gagarin had been able to sleep during his space flight around the earth.

We thought that our subjects would spend a great deal of time in "looking" about, becoming adjusted to S.D., reflecting upon his impressions of S.D., reacting to the stress generated by such isolation. Apparently, however, the subjects even at the outset attended to none of these features of the confinement, but rather responded to its monotony, and there can be no doubt that S.D. is the acme of monotony. Their reaction to this boredom was to make the best possible adjustment —to shut it out by going to sleep. It was a very effective technique; it was not, however, a deliberate act. They did not in effect say, "This is boring, so I'm going to sleep." The sleep came quickly and automatically. Such an adjustment is known to us all, for it is used by everyone in boring situations. In the present case sleep was probably facilitated by the conditions of darkness and quietness which are present in our normal sleeping experiences.

As the confinement time increased, sleep was less easy to come by. The subject tended to accumulate all the sleep he could, and thus one avenue of escape from boredom was taken from him. When this happened, which was in the second day of confinement, he was forced to become more resourceful to cope with S.D. It will be seen later, in Chapter VI, that the initial sleep can be prevented, in most cases, if the subject is given some very simple task to perform, one as simple as pushing a button at the end of what he estimates to be one hour, for each waking hour will suffice to eliminate most of the initial sleep. In a similar manner the subject could invent tasks to relieve the tedium. As we shall see, most successful subjects did just that.

It would be a mistake to overemphasize the monotony of S.D., for it was not such to *all* subjects. There were some who were rather neutral about S.D., some who mildly disliked it, and one or two who actively enjoyed it. For some it provided a period of rest—a rather constant need for most students. For others it provided a period of tranquillity during which meditation came easily. And for others it afforded a period of productive mental activity.

The most striking case of a subject who enjoyed S.D. was one who upon release *requested* an additional day or so of confinement. Many subjects had indicated upon release that they could have endured another day or even more, but no one had yet requested additional confinement time. Naturally we fell upon this subject with a host of questions. At first he said that he liked the food and rest and wanted more. He even offered to do the additional time free of charge; he wasn't motivated by the money. After a while we finally got at his real reason for liking S.D., and it was very sensible. He had used his confinement time in a very meaningful way by practicing what he was sure was going to happen to him later in life. He was from Turkey and was in the United States studying politics. He was convinced that when he returned to Turkey he would get into difficulties over political matters and probably end up a political prisoner in solitary confinement at some time in his life. Thus he was practicing an adjustment to this in S.D. I think he was enthusiastic about S.D. because he was relieved to find that he could easily endure such a test.

EFFECTS OF INTERRUPTION

It is generally agreed that we do not ordinarily relish interruptions. There is some evidence to suggest that if we are performing a task we resent interruptions even when the work is not necessarily pleasant. However, it is a common finding with most people that an interruption of very unpleasant activity is very desirable. Common sense tells us so, and from it we could predict that almost any interruption in S.D. would be desirable. But such was not the case.

In one series of studies, to be discussed in Part III, we interrupted S.D. every twelve hours to conduct some learning tests—simple rote memory tasks and as such not entirely distasteful, but never pleasant, either. Nevertheless we predicted that the interruption would provide such a break in the monotony as to be greatly anticipated and enjoyed by the subject. But, far from finding it a welcome relief, the subjects reported that they greatly resented our intrusions. It was natural that they would not enjoy doing a learning task—we can all remember mild distaste for memorizing poetry and the like—but their resentment was greater than mild distaste—they were irritated and resentful. One subject expressed the feeling very well when he said, "It was another way of viewing the old saying 'Misery loves company.' We cared not for your company since you did not share our misery."

Apparently the interruptions not only failed to bring relief to the monotony, but also served as a subtle reminder that more was yet to come. The breaks also tended to prevent adjustment to the conditions of S.D. because each caused the subject to begin S.D. all over again and without the benefit of escape by initial sleep.

Most of the subjects arrived at another reason for resenting the interruptions. Almost every subject independently decided that, among other things, we were studying the effects of S.D. upon their ability to keep track of time. They all felt that the intervals between interruptions were not *equally spaced* (they actually were) and hence were a deliberate attempt on our part to mislead them. They did not view the intervals as becoming increasingly longer or shorter, but merely randomly different.

I should point out here that, although we had no such objective at the outset, the reports of these subjects helped to convince us that we should study the effects of S.D. upon man's ability to judge time. The results of that study are in Chapter VI.

MENTAL ACTIVITIES

During the waking phases of S.D. every subject reported a constant preoccupation with mental effort. Some engaged in extensive daydreaming and some in active problem solving; all of our subjects came to us with the intent to engage in creative thinking. As indicated, our subjects were graduate students and as such had plenty of academic problems to work out. Most of them looked forward to S.D. as a period when they could devote full time and maximum effort to such activities. Many, however, found that they could not maintain thought during S.D. and so they drifted in reverie over which they had little control. One subject claimed that it was like having his mind in "freewheeling." More of this will be discussed later.

AUTOMATIC AIR-CONDITIONING

As our subjects described what S.D. was like, there was one unusual observation that occurred with regularity. Their claim was that as confinement continued the air became hot, humid, and stale, and that they experienced an oppressive atmosphere that frequently produced headaches. Then the subjects would go to sleep, and when they awoke would find the room cool, the air fresh, and the headaches gone, leading most of them to believe that we had replenished the cubicle air while they slept. This was not the case.

The report of the cool air may be related to what the

human body does by way of generating heat under different conditions. A man seated at rest will generate about 400 BTU's per hour, whereas if he goes to sleep he will generate about 275 BTU's per hour. Hence during sleep less heat was liberated to the air within the cubicle, which was perceived by the subject upon awaking as a cooler room. That this is not actually the case was indicated by a remote-reading thermometer located in the cubicle and read in the experimenter's room. The room starts out at 70° F. and gradually climbs, within twelve hours, to 76° F., where it remains for the duration of the confinement. The thermometer never shows any changes after it reaches stability of greater than about ½° F., which hardly seems enough to explain the subject's reaction.

We have measured the body temperature of a subject and have found that it drops a few tenths of a degree during sleep. We made this discovery after deciding to photograph a subject during S.D. to determine his positions and movements, a procedure that was clearly out of the question until I learned of a special camera from Mr. William Pain, of the *Life* magazine staff. This remarkable camera, called an Evapograph,* takes pictures of infrared radiations, and of course the heat liberated by the human body is just that kind of radiation. Hence it is possible to "take a picture" in total darkness of the heat image of any object that

*The camera is a product of the Baird Atomic Company of Cambridge, Mass. Interested persons should inquire through Mr. Potter Trainer of that company.

gives off infrared radiation. With this arrangement we took pictures at half-hour intervals of a subject confined for twenty-four hours, and obtained a record of his heat image. The color of the picture was then translated into degrees, and the results revealed the expected temperature drop during sleep.

The heat-image pictures revealed one finding that was, as far as I know, new and unusual. The body temperature did decrease during sleep, but the temperature of the head did not. I suppose that we should have expected to discover this, since it is an established fact that the blood volume of the brain increases during sleep, and presumably this could counteract any cooling effect and thus maintain normal temperature of the head throughout sleep.

CONTROL OF CUBICLE AIR

It would have been ideal to air-condition the cubicle in order to maintain a constant temperature as well as a constant supply of fresh air. The construction of the room was such, however, that to do so would have been prohibitively expensive or would have violated the soundproof condition of the room. Thus we were confronted with the problem of getting rid of the subject's expired carbon dioxide and yet not violating the conditions of S.D. A somewhat similar problem occurs on submarines, though the undersea craft can use reconverters with little consideration for noise.

The submarine literature on the problem of CO_2 elimination gave us an answer. We had measured the oxygen level and the CO_2 level of the confinement cubicle during a forty-eight-hour confinement. From this we discovered that there was plenty of O_2 present at the end of forty-eight hours and, by extrapolation, even at the end of ninety-six hours. The problem was the accumulation of CO_2, which was higher than the recommended industrial minimum after forty-eight hours. The solution to the problem was to eliminate chemically the undesirable CO_2. As CO_2 is heavy, it sank to the floor, where we eliminated it by absorption. Sodium hydroxide crystals, placed in trays beneath the bed, readily absorbed the CO_2, so that there was not a measurable trace of it after forty-eight hours of confinement. The chemical absorption of the CO_2 was an ideal solution to the problem because the process did not produce noise, odor, or harmful gases. It is caustic, however, so the trays were covered with screen lids. The subjects were informed of the trays and told to avoid any contact with them. Perhaps a better solution would have been to absorb the CO_2 by potassium superoxide, which not only eliminates CO_2 but also liberates O_2.

SOME HEALTH ITEMS

Three of our subjects who came to the laboratory to start S.D. had the beginnings of bad head and chest colds. Our first reaction was to send them away, but later appointments could not be worked out, and, as we never had an easy time enlisting subjects, they were accepted, colds and all. They were confined for forty-eight hours, and when they were released from S.D. not one had a trace of a cold. All three expressed amazement at the rapid recovery, since it was their usual experience to keep colds for a week or so rather than for two days, and especially since they had had no medication.

We can only assume that the very complete rest afforded by S.D. was responsible for the rapid recovery from the colds. This may suggest that S.D. as a form of complete rest, in conjunction with proper medication, could effect recoveries more rapidly than if one merely went to bed during illness. Dr. Azima, of the Montreal Neurological Institute, has attempted such treatment for mental patients. It is his claim that S.D. brings about a more rapid personalization process in the patient than would be otherwise possible.

In one of our early studies we restricted the movements of our subjects somewhat by placing cardboard gauntlets on their arms. The gauntlet extended from above the elbow to beyond the finger tips and was held in place by a wrist cuff. We found that the gauntlet was not necessary in order to restrict movement of our subjects, so its use was later discarded, but in the case of two subjects it was of extreme importance. Both of these men came to us with severe cases of poison ivy. Obviously we would not have allowed them to serve as S.D. subjects had we known, but, as it turned out, both men were completely cured at the end of their confinement, which for one was forty-eight hours, and for the other seventy-two hours. Thinking back on it, I do not see how they endured that situation, for the gauntlets so covered their hands they could not scratch, and, also, they had been asked to lie still. To be sure, each could have pulled off the gauntlets and scratched to his heart's content and we would have been none the wiser. But both men insisted that they carried out our instructions to the letter, that at no time did they scratch their itching poison ivy, for they felt to do so would be contrary to our instructions to lie as quietly as possible. It may not be surprising that the poison ivy was cured in such a short time; medical counsel indicates that this affliction, if not most skin diseases, can be readily cured merely by not scratching the affected areas. It is very surprising, however, that our two subjects could resist scratching. Both men claimed that it was easy to resist scratching *because* of S.D. Apparently they both felt that the itching sensation was a welcome relief in circumstances devoid of stimulation. It is of interest that a sensation such as an itch, which normally is very insistent, can be viewed so differently during S.D., and that even normally unpleasant sensations may during S.D. become desirable for the simple reason that they tend to relieve monotony. Does this suggest that monotony is even more undesirable than we imagine?

Similar to the reactions of these two subjects is the manner in which many of them behaved in another situation. Fully three quarters of our subjects were smokers, and they were not allowed to smoke during S.D. When they were told of this prohibition, they predicted that nonsmoking would be the hardest aspect of the confinement. But to a man it turned out to be the *easiest* part of S.D. They all reported that they seldom thought about smoking and that when they did it was as a mere memory and not the demanding insistence of an old habit. Some of these people were confined for as long as ninety-six hours, and, as any smoker will testify, it is not a simple matter to give up smoking for four days.

Our first reaction was to say that they did not desire to smoke because, being in the dark, they would not enjoy visually the act of smoking. But, as many blind people smoke and as many people do smoke in the dark, that is hardly the full answer. I might add here in this regard, however, that Professor Clark Hull, a psychologist, demonstrated the importance of vision for smoking. He found that blindfolded smokers were unable to distinguish between a pipe full of tobacco and one merely filled with *warm air!*

Not only did the absence of light in S.D. help our subjects not to think about smoking, but there was also the absence of social facilitation, obviously an important factor to smoking. These two factors would, at first, seem to explain the ease of giving up smoking during S.D. But, on the other hand, S.D. should be just the situation to increase the need to smoke, for, as we are led to believe, under stress and strain one smokes more, and surely S.D. was so stressful that our subjects should have been more aware of the urge to smoke.

Smoking is such a powerful habit, such a difficult one to break; and for those who have attempted to break the habit the first few days are usually very trying. Though I find the effect of S.D. on it hard to explain, one thought does intrude itself. Our subjects did not *intend* to break the smoking habit; they were merely putting it aside for a few days. In general we can tolerate unpleasant events if we know that they have a definite termination. Perhaps our subjects found it easy to do without smoking because they knew that they would soon return to it. And they did! That they started smoking again after release from S.D. surprises me. The present concern over the relation between smoking and lung cancer has made most people consider breaking the habit, and, when we had gotten these men by as many as four days of not smoking, it is a wonder that they returned to it. Perhaps their abstinence had come too easily to effect a permanent cure.

The amazing effects of S.D. on such a commanding habit as smoking leads us to speculate on other habits. Are less dominant habits more easily disrupted by

S.D.? If one desired to break the habit, say, of nail biting, would he more likely succeed if he began in S.D.? And what about habitual ways of thinking? If the desire of nicotine addiction can be altered by S.D., what are the chances of altering political, moral, or ethical desires by S.D.? The reader may feel that this is too big a jump, that nicotine addiction is physiological and that morals or political affiliations are mental. But perhaps the jump is not so great as we imagine. It is reasonable to believe, and many do, that in the last analysis mental acts such as thinking are really physiological. Action we call thought may be the electrical and chemical activity of brain cells. And if this is the case, it is then not unreasonable to expect to influence these actions by physical conditions. In any event, let us give this idea a trial in the next section.

S.D. AND BRAINWASHING

Brainwashing, as it was practiced a few short years ago, was simply a process of rapidly altering a person's beliefs, usually about political matters. Education is really a slow, long-term form of brainwashing. If we wish to teach a group of people a particular belief or attitude about, say, politics or religion, and if these people are available to us from birth, we educate them. With these conditions we can raise children to believe any way we desire. We can make them devout Catholics or convinced atheists, liberals or conservatives, Communists or Democrats, Buddhists or Baptists; it is all a matter of training. The Communists have wanted, in many situations, to train people along certain lines of political belief, but they have not always had control over these people since birth. They are often people who have fallen under Communist domination and they have to be subjected to "forceful indoctrination" —they have to be brainwashed. With plenty of time and early control man can teach man anything by education, but without time and early control he may teach by brainwashing. Thus I think we can see that brainwashing is not some new horror invented in the mid-twentieth century, but a technique that has been with us for a long time. It seems dramatic because of the startling conversions it has produced.

In the beginning of Communist brainwashing activity there were many people to be brainwashed and few to do the washing. Thus some were confined to long prison terms prior to being subjected to the process. It soon became obvious to the captors that there were more and easier conversions from those people who were imprisoned, and especially if they were in solitary confinement prior to the forceful indoctrination. Thus solitary confinement became a routine prelude to brainwashing—the "softening-up" period, as it was called. It is not hard to imagine how effective such treatment could be.

In a very recent study conducted in our laboratories

by Dr. Suedfeld, the effect of S.D. upon susceptibility to propaganda was measured. We attempted to produce attitude change favorable to Turkey in people whose attitude was originally neutral. A special test of attitude was used to select subjects with neutral views. Incidentally, this was no problem since most of those tested met the requirement.

One half of the subjects were confined under the most severe conditions of S.D. for twenty-four hours. The other half were permitted to engage in relatively unrestricted activity such as reading, walking about the building, going to a movie, etc., for the same period of time.

At the end of the twenty-four hours each subject heard a tape which contained propaganda favorable to Turkey. All subjects, regardless of previous treatment, heard the tape in the S.D. cubicle so that everyone received the propaganda under the same conditions. Immediately after they had heard the tape their attitudes toward Turkey were once again assessed. It was found that those subjects who were confined evidenced attitude change favorable to Turkey. The change was statistically significant. There was however, no significant change in the attitudes of the nonconfined group. The average change of the S.D. group was over eight times as large as that of the nonconfined group. These data will be presented in more detail a little further on in this section. We may conclude that the effects of S.D.

are similar to those of brainwashing. That is to say, confinement rendered people more susceptible to propaganda and led to greater attitude change.

It is obviously impossible to make direct comparisons between our S.D. work and brainwashing. Our subjects were volunteers, who could leave the chamber at will. They underwent no physical hardships, the period of confinement was short, and the experience was not fear-arousing. It should also be pointed out that the attitude under consideration was one about which the subjects had no strong feelings, whereas in the real brainwashing situation the propaganda may be directed against cherished beliefs. There are, nonetheless, common elements of S.D. and the softening-up period of brainwashing that suggest comparisons.

In the softening-up process and in S.D. the confined individual experiences dreadful monotony and boredom, so much so that he will actively seek almost any form of novelty. If we wished, for some obscure reason, to develop a superior brainwashing system, we could turn this quest for novelty to our advantage. Assume that we wish to instill a particular belief in a person. Assume, for example, that we wished to convert this individual to Islam, a belief we knew to be repulsive to him, but one about which he knew very little. Let us further assume that he holds very strongly to a Protestant belief about which he also understands very little. To "convert" him, the best procedure would be: First, place him in S.D. for four days in order to get him receptive to novelty—any novelty. At the end of four days introduce two switches without any instruction into the cubicle. If he operated Switch A, he would hear a thirty-second speech favoring his brand of Protestantism. If he operated Switch B, he would hear a thirty-second speech favoring Islam. The main difference between the two switches is that Switch A always produces the *same* speech, whereas Switch B always produces a *different* one and always by a different voice. In this manner the monotony of S.D. would become associated with the monotony of the repetitious speech on Protestantism, and the desire for novelty would lead to the selection of Switch B. Now arrange the switches so that he can operate them less often, and our battle is practically won. We have caused this individual, by *his own choice,* to listen to our propaganda. If we can get him to listen, we can get him to believe by making our propaganda clever enough.

Although America has never used such a technique and presumably never will, there can be no doubt that we could build a very effective brainwashing technique. Dr. Hebb and his people at McGill University have already demonstrated that, with techniques similar to those described, confined individuals will spend much more time listening to a variety of unfavored items than to the same favored item.

If our hypothetical prisoner had insisted upon a repetition of Switch A, this too could work in our favor, for repetition can weaken meaning. We have all experienced what happens to a word when we repeat it over and over. Its sound becomes strange to us, as though it were a new word. We still know the definition of the word, but it has changed, its meaning has been weakened. It seems reasonable to believe that something similar to this process could happen as a result of a repetition of slogans.

The Red Chinese used this trick in the brainwashing activity in Korea. They often required U.N. prisoners to write an autobiography. When it was completed they required that it be written again without benefit of the previous copy, and again, and so on for countless times until the prisoner was extremely bored with that activity. The Chinese probably did not realize that it was the monotonous repetition that was weakening some of the soldiers' cherished beliefs; they were only looking for discrepancies in the reports. These were considered to be signs of weak areas and consequently the logical focus of their psychological attack to convert the prisoner to communism.

But back to our hypothetical prisoner. Once we have him listening to our propaganda, we should then reward any evidences of conversion. For example, we might occasionally ask questions about Islam. This should be done over an intercommunication system so as not to interrupt S.D. visually. If he gives the proper answers to our questions, he should be rewarded, perhaps by a little light. Later, if his answers get better, we might introduce a novel food item to replace a highly repetitious diet, and still later we might reward his answers by social contacts. Again note that a similar process was used by the Red Chinese. In the indoctrination process when a prisoner said a "proper" thing he often received a candy bar. These responses are forthcoming from the individual and not forced out of him by pain or punishment, thereby making them more nearly his own beliefs.

Incidentally I would *guess* that the less intelligent our prisoner, the less likely we are to convert him. The duller intellect would probably plod along more content merely to hear repetitions of his own belief than the brighter individual, who needs more material to feed his intellect. On the other hand the "conversion" of our more intelligent prisoner probably would be less permanent. Once released from our control, he is more likely to reason through the process and understand his "conversion." If he understands he can easily reinstate his old belief by a technique similar to that used in his conversion.

To be sure, our hypothetical case would not convert everyone, but very likely it could be a much more effective system than has been used to date.

Repulsive as these procedures may seem, it is not too early to realize that we must study these phenomena and techniques if we are to have defenses against them. It is also necessary to realize that in one way or another we are all brainwashers. The mother who teaches her child is molding a particular set of beliefs and attitudes. The teacher also places, although probably much less effectively, a certain cant to the beliefs of students. And so on through all the progenitors of a given culture. This is the natural system by which one acquires his beliefs, in contrast to the forceful-indoctrination system. The natural system is not free from force, however; it is only that the force is spread out and applied slowly and gradually so that it is not always detected. In brainwashing the force is applied more rapidly, but note that in our "improved" brainwashing system the forces are fairly subtle, and except for the obvious confinement they may not be detectable.

At this point one should justify suggesting a technique whereby something as horrible as a superior brainwashing method could evolve; for, if man is ever again to encounter brainwashing, he must understand it in order to protect himself against it. For example, if it is known that a particular individual is very susceptible to the effect of S.D., then his military assignment should be such as to decrease his chances of capture. If he is nevertheless captured but knows what to expect from the process, he can eliminate the element of surprise and reduce the effectiveness of the unknown. He will have in advance not only knowledge of what treatment to expect but knowledge of what to expect from himself.

The importance of individual differences was clearly shown in the previously mentioned study involving propaganda about Turkey. The personality characteristic considered was concreteness-abstractness. This refers to the manner in which one makes use of information. For example, one who accepts information at face value without considering his own knowledge and experience may be said to be concrete. On the other hand, under the same circumstance, the abstract individual would evaluate the information, utilizing his total experience, present and past.

Furthermore, the concrete individual needs extended information and feels stressed when it is lacking, whereas the abstract individual is more self reliant.[1]

It may be that man's ability to wage warfare has moved ahead so fast that brainwashing is already old-fashioned. There may be no need for brainwashing if total war is so effective as to leave no prisoners to convert or no country to occupy. At present, however, we are not in a total war but are instead witness to many limited wars, and as long as these exist there will be prisoners and occupation, and possibly some form of forceful indoctrination.

Therefore, we would predict that the concrete individual would be more stressed by S.D. and hence more influenced by whatever information is provided. In

---

[1] *Conceptual Systems and Personality Organization by* O. J. Harvey, D. E. Hunt and H. M. Schroder. New York: Wiley, 1961.

comparison, abstract subjects should be less susceptible to propaganda presentations.

In the study under consideration, personality tests were used to identify and select concrete, abstract, and intermediate individuals. As expected, we found that the concrete individuals showed greater attitude change in the direction of the propaganda than either of the other two types of individuals. See table below.

Average Attitude Change

	S.D.	Non-confined	System Average
Concrete	32%	10%	21%
Intermediate	18%	3%	11%
Abstract	8%	– 6%*	1%
Treatment Average	20%	3%	

*A negative score means that these subjects change their attitudes opposite to that of the propaganda, i.e., became less favorable toward Turkey.

In summary, these data suggest that personality differences significantly affect reactions in the brainwashing situations.

PART TWO

Sensory Deprivation and Its Effect Upon Some Mental Abilities

CHAPTER III

Are There Dreams in S.D.?

THE SUBJECT of dreams as investigated by us is not adequate material for a scientific study and is not offered here as such. Dreams are highly subjective reports that are impossible to check upon.* Nevertheless dreams are fascinating occurrences that in the present case may reveal something about the ways our subjects reacted to S.D. Some investigators who study dreams believe that the dream sequence is almost always related to some recent event. Thus, because S.D. subjects have experienced a great reduction in the number and variety of prior events, we came to inquire about their dreams. The following accounts are of dreams that occurred during S.D. I have also taken the liberty of offering some interpretations of the

---

*Recently the occurrence of dreams has been objectively determined by the simple procedure of observing eye movements. Dr. Eugene Aserinsky has discovered that we use scanning eye movement during dreams much as we would use viewing any scene. With such an indicator it has been possible to do fascinating work with dreams; the interested reader is referred to an article by Dr. Nathaniel Kleitman entitled "The Problem of Dreams," in *Scientific American,* November, 1960, pp. 82-88.

dreams; the reader should understand, however, that any dream has many possible interpretations.

The meanings of some of the dreams were specially clear to me, the following example being a good case in point. In his dream our subject was going swimming with four friends. On the way to the pool he bragged a great deal about his swimming and diving ability. His claims met with a great deal of skepticism from his companions, and he was challenged to prove his claims. Upon arriving at the pool he was unable to prove his assertions because he had forgotten to bring his swimming trunks. At this point he awoke. We had planned to confine this subject for ninety-six hours, but he pushed the panic button after twenty-six hours of S.D. His dream seems to contain elements of defeat not unlike his actual one by S.D. He, like most subjects who pushed the panic button, considered the requesting of an early release to be an act of defeat or failure.

In his dream the four friends and four days of S.D. may have been related. He did not know that we had planned to keep him in the cubicle for four days, but he knew of a previous subject who had been confined for that period.

One of our subjects pushed the panic button as a direct result of a dream. He dreamed that he saw his wife driving from his home to the S.D. laboratory to pick him up. In the dream she had departed from home shortly after he entered confinement. (Did he know even in his dream that he was going to demand an early release from S.D.?) As she drove to the laboratory he saw her car traveling on a collision course with a truck. At this point he awoke before he could determine how the dream turned out. He was unable to stop thinking about the dream, and the uncertainty about the "accident" caused him, in his words, to push the panic button. This particular subject is convinced that he is capable of prophetic dreams and has had what he considers to be two very dramatic proofs of his ability. And so it is understandable that, as he said, he "simply had to know whether or not the accident had occurred." He called his wife from the laboratory, and, although she was all right, he would not allow her to drive over to pick him up.

His demand for an early release came shortly after forty-eight hours of S.D., indicating that he could take a fair amount of confinement. There is little doubt that he could have taken more had it not been for his dream. In fact he offered to return to the cubicle any time we needed him. I feel that this man is blameless for having responded to his dream. We have all experienced the confusion that comes after awaking from a very dramatic dream. We often spend some time before we separate real life from the dream state, and, since even the waking condition of S.D. is very like that of sleep, it is no wonder that he felt some compulsions about his dream.

Another subject reported that because of his dreams

he was forced to push the panic button. While in S.D. he had frequent and very violent dreams, occurrences that were not at all normal for him. He could not describe the dreams beyond saying that they were merely a hodgepodge of frightful events strung together in no logical series. This scrambled array of horror was so unbearable to this man that he attempted to remain awake to avoid it. Naturally he wasn't entirely successful, and, when he found that he could not prevent sleeping and consequently dreaming, he pushed the button for release. In our opinion S.D. was doing something to him that caused his dreams to be very threatening. It may be enough to say that he found S.D. unpleasant and that his feelings were most vividly expressed by his dreams. He did the only sensible thing he could, which was to get out of S.D.

The dream of another subject clearly illustrates the confusion that occurs when one awakes from a dream. In his dream this man had a headache that became intense. He dreamed that he pushed the panic button because of his headache. When the experimenter came in (in his dream), he mentioned his headache and the experimenter gave him a bottle of aspirin and told him to continue the confinement. Later the subject awoke with an actual headache, whereupon he reached up to the shelf, fully confident of finding aspirin there. It was something of a shock to him to discover no shelf and no aspirin. While puzzling over this and considering his dream, his headache became more severe and, just as in his dream, he pushed the panic button. Upon releasing this subject we could not meet his request for aspirin but promised him some at the finish of the postconfinement tests. Long before the tests were completed he noted that his headache was gone.

Not all of the dreams came from subjects who pushed the panic button. The subjects who successfully completed their stay in S.D. also dreamed. Many of their dreams were about sexual matters, which, as they indicated, were also often the subject matter of their daydreams.

One subject started to report his dream in this manner: ". . . my confinement dreams were not in color, which is usual for me, since I never dream in color." We asked why he thought to mention it. A very puzzled look came over his face, and then he said, "Wait a minute! One of my dreams was in color, at least part of it was." He then went on to relate that in his dream he was outside the apartment house of his girl friend. Then he found himself standing in the hallway at the foot of the stairs that led up to her apartment. Along the balustrade she had hung the various articles of her clothing. It was her clothing that was colored.

On the surface this dream seems innocent enough and reveals nothing but possibly the untidy habits of his girl friend. However, when one refers this dream to a Freudian interpretation, we find a classic textbook account of sexual dream symbolism. According to Freud, dreams of ladders, stairs, and the like are symbolic representations of the act of sexual intercourse. His argument is straightforward; in climbing ladders and stairs there are rhythmical intervals, with increasing breathlessness, until finally one reaches the height. The height, in turn, becomes a position from which one can easily descend. Thus it appears, if one accepts Freud's ideas, that in a neatly disguised and socially acceptable form our subject had dreamed of a sexual act with his girl friend. It is interesting to note that in his dream she had no need to disguise her desire, and so in a forthright manner she appropriately, if somewhat impatiently, abandoned her clothes. There is another interesting item here—logically she would remove her clothes in the bedroom and not on the stairs, but his dream symbolism apparently will not allow him in her bedroom. Thus in order to protect his integrity his dream utilizes a staircase where it is innocent enough for him to stand, but upon which the dream allows his lady fair to act as a wanton wench. I am sure he does not consciously regard her in such a manner, but in order to protect him the dream state is quick to sacrifice her.

Evidently this dream impressed him, for later he dreamed of going to church, that he was late arriving at church because he couldn't find a place to park. When he finally found a parking place his automobile turned into a wheel, which he could have easily parked anywhere or even taken into church with him. Because he was late getting into church all the hymn books were "used up" and so he was unable to sing. This disappointed him greatly and at this point he awoke.

We asked this subject if he saw any relationship between the two dreams. He not only saw no relationship, he was unable to explain either dream.

Stairs appeared in the dreams of other subjects. Sometimes the subject dreamed that he was walking up a flight of stairs, in some cases with a woman and in some cases alone. One subject dreamed of standing at the head of some stairs and seeing horrible things, but he was unable to say what they were.

Many have reported that while in S.D. they often found that they were thinking back over childhood memories. That this should happen is not surprising, for S.D. has many elements that are similar to childhood. As in childhood our subjects are dependent upon others for food and protection. The experimenter clearly exercises a position of authority over the subject. Not only are some of the conditions reminiscent of childhood, but there is ample time and nothing to do, and it is only natural that vivid memories should occur.

One subject reflected a childhood experience by dreaming of animals. All of his dreams had jungle themes, and he was constantly falling into lions' dens, snake pits, tiger traps, and the like. He did not find the dreams particularly frightening, but he was unable to "shake them off." Finally these dreams brought back with vivid clarity a childhood experience. He remembered that as a very young boy he had been prevented from getting out of bed by a nurse who told him that there was a tiger beneath his bed. She told him that as long as he was in bed he was safe, but should he swing his legs over the edge of the bed to the floor the tiger would bite them. Apparently that had proved very effective, and he said that even since he had become an adult the memory had an element of fear for him. After he had remembered the experience with the nurse and while he was still in S.D., he had the persistent thought "Maybe there is a tiger in here with me." He knew that the idea was ridiculous, but he could not dismiss it.

The theme of pits occurred in the dreams of another subject. This is not surprising when you consider that being in S.D. is somewhat like being trapped in a pit. This particular subject had several dreams in which the only detail he could recall was a pit of some sort. In one dream he drove a car into a pit of mud. In another he drove a tank into a pit of sand. In his dreams he struggled unsuccessfully to get out of the pits. He was disturbed by his dreams, but not enough to make him push the panic button.

A childhood theme was expressed by the dream of another subject. According to Freud, to dream of flying like a bird is symbolic of returning to childhood. He reasons that children are often held high in the air by adult friends and family and swung around much like a bird. Our subject dreamed that he was standing by a lake watching others in a motorboat. (Children often see others as having all the fun.) He asked for a ride in the boat. (Children are seldom reluctant to state their desires.) His request was denied on the grounds that the boat was out of gas. (Children are so often denied their requests.) In order to prove that gasoline was unnecessary he took off and flew jet-propelled over the lake. (The reveries of children often make them the greatest of heroes.) When he returned to the shore he nearly landed on the head of a spectator in the crowd that had gathered to watch him, and this so amused him that he awoke laughing. (The humor of children often favors slapstick.)

One of our subjects spent most of his time in S.D. outlining articles and reports he planned to write. This sort of activity seems to have influenced his dream material. In his dream he was employed by the *Daily Mirror* as a foreign reporter in the Middle East. He was born in Baghdad. In the dream he was reading a propaganda leaflet emphasizing the nonaggressive nature of Iraq's foreign policy. As he read the leaflet, it suddenly turned into an A. & P. grocery advertisement. This dream seems to be pure caprice unless it represents his opinion of American foreign policy. It would not be surprising to find that a person from the Middle East regarded the United States, with all its surplus food, as an A. & P. advertisement. In any event, the dream is probably unrelated to S.D.

Another subject dreamed that he was guarding some

money while traveling on a train, and that some people in the next *compartment* stole the money. At first he planned to take the money back, but then he reasoned that "she" would only steal it again. He waited until just before the train arrived before taking the money, and in this manner there was not enough time for it to be stolen for the second time.

This dream contains many elements of S.D. The subject on the train was in a compartment; S.D. was in a small cubicle. On the train he was guarding money, and in S.D. he was being paid. That the money should be stolen is close to the attitude most subjects had toward their pay, namely, that when one considered the task at hand, it was so low as to be close to robbery. In the dream he was almost helpless to prevent the robbery, somewhat reflecting the control of the experimenter over the subject.

Except for the cases indicated, our S.D. subjects enjoyed their dreams, even tried to induce them, since they came as welcome breaks in the tedium. Some of them carried their dreams over into daydreams, thus helping to pass the waking time and serving as a fairly effective means of doing so.

CHAPTER IV

Effects of S.D. on Suggestibility

IN CHAPTER II the role of confinements as a softening-up process was discussed. At that time the process was related to the changing of a belief or an attitude. Another way of discussing a similar problem is to show the effect of confinement on suggestibility, the general notion being that isolation and confinement render one more agreeable to suggestion.

The McGill studies made some pertinent findings. They tested their subjects' attitudes toward the supernatural—ghosts, poltergeists, clairvoyance, mediums, etc. As might be expected, most of the subjects held fairly negative beliefs about these phenomena. They were then placed in confinement where specially prepared propaganda on behalf of the supernatural was presented by a tape recorder. After confinement a retest of their beliefs revealed that they had changed their attitudes in favor of this material. The same propaganda used on a nonconfined comparison group of subjects proved ineffective. Thus the McGill work found that S.D. increased the acceptance of a special kind of propaganda, possibly another way of saying that S.D. rendered those subjects more suggestible.

We set out in a different way to measure the degree to which S.D. would influence suggestion. The first test we used was a modification of that devised by Alfred Binet, the French psychologist known for his innovation in testing human intelligence. We presented line drawings of various designs.

They were presented *one at a time* and very briefly —1/100 of a second. After each presentation the subject was given thirty seconds to reproduce as accurately as possible what he had seen. The test was administered in the laboratory area outside the confinement cubicle and was given only at the end of the confinement period. The subjects had no advance knowledge of the test.

The designs were arranged in a series that had a special ordering of circles. At first the circles were closed, then they had a slight gap that became systematically larger as the series continued. All the other figures had no gaps; thus there was the *suggestion* that *all* of the figures had no gaps. This suggestion should have the effect of causing the gaps in the circles to be detected only after the gap had become quite large. We predicted that the S.D. subject would be more influenced by the suggestion and thus would not detect as small a gap in the circles as would a nonconfined group of subjects. As it turned out, the S.D. subjects detected the gap a little better than did the comparison subjects. However, the S.D. group did reveal a strong increase in suggestibility that we did not expect. After they detected the gaps in the circles, they started drawing gaps in the other figures as well. There was a total of 110 figures presented, of which 25 were the circles. Of the remaining figures the S.D. group saw 23, on the average, as having gaps, while the nonconfined group saw none. We had instructed both groups to draw as accurately as possible what they saw; apparently the S.D. group responded more nearly to our instructions, for we found that some of the figures without gaps had slight imperfections in them, owing to the slide-mounting process. The S.D. subjects picked up these imperfections, while the other group did not. We contend that this suggestion was a very subtle one and that it had more influence on S.D. subjects than on the nonconfined subjects.

The above suggestion is more subtle than direct verbal commands. Consequently we arranged a test to determine the effectiveness of more direct and possibly stronger suggestion upon S.D. subjects. In this instance we used the well-known "body-sway" technique, which demonstrates that it is difficult to stand erect with the eyes closed and with feet together without swaying. It is also true that while one is trying to stand he can be influenced to sway more if the proper commands are given. If he is told that he is moving, say, backward, he will counteract by moving forward even if he was standing perfectly still at the time. It is easy to see how this technique offered a way of measuring suggestibility. All we had to do was to measure how much each person swayed without any suggestions given to him ("normal sway"), and then how much he swayed when suggestion was continually present ("suggested sway"). The difference between the two would be a measure of the effectiveness of the suggestion, or, said differently, it would be a measure of the suggestibility of the individual.

We reasoned that the effectiveness of the suggestion telling the individual to sway would be greater after S.D. than before, and we proceeded as follows: The subject was placed on a small platform two inches high, with his toes slightly over the edge. He was blindfolded, his feet were placed together, his arms were placed by his side, and he was instructed to stand as erect and as still as possible. He was left standing this way for two minutes ten seconds.* A lightweight plastic band was fitted snugly around his head. To the back and to the side of the band fine threads were attached. These threads led to recording pens, and each movement made by the subject produced a reaction in the appropriate pen, which wrote upon a moving roll of paper.

The "suggested" body-sway test was conducted in the same fashion, except that throughout the period of two minutes ten seconds the following suggestions were given to him by the experimenter. "You are to imagine

*The time of two minutes ten seconds was used because the identical amount of time was necessary for the suggestion-to-sway used in the next part of the experiment.

that you are standing on the edge at the top of a very tall skyscraper. The wind is blowing at your back. In fact you are leaning forward—stand up straight. Not too much. You are now leaning back. Stand perfectly still and up straight, not over to the right. You are still leaning to the right and now a little forward; stand erect. The wind is blowing very hard now, don't bend over . . ."

The table below provides the data gathered by the body-sway experiment. The figures represent the total amount of sway in millimeters accumulated during each period that sway was measured. The S.D. confinement was for seventy-two hours.

	Pre-S.D.	Post-S.D.	Post-S.D. plus 48 Hours
Normal Sway	280	287	249
Suggested Sway	294	338	245
Difference	14	51	–4

The measurements before S.D. show that on the average our subjects were slightly influenced by suggestion. By talking to them we could effect only a 5 per cent increase in their body sway. Notice, however, that when the same test is conducted after seventy-two hours of S.D. the effectiveness of the suggestion increases. At this point the increase in sway is almost four times greater than before S.D. The last column represents measurements we made two days after each subject was released from S.D. It is easy to see that they have lost their heightened suggestibility. These data seem to say that it can be increased by S.D. but that the change is not permanent and is entirely lost after release from confinement.

We next came to ask if it was necessary to place a subject in S.D. for as long as seventy-two hours in order to effect the increase in his suggestibility, and so we measured other groups of subjects, who were confined for either one or two days. Aside from the length of confinement the procedure was the same as that above. The people confined for only twenty-four hours showed *no* increase in suggestibility: if anything, they were less suggestible after twenty-four hours of S.D. than before. Those confined for forty-eight hours showed increased suggestibility after S.D., and, as in the case of those confined for seventy-two hours, the sway was more than three times greater after S.D. Thus we probably may conclude that forty-eight hours of S.D. is nearly as effective as seventy-two hours in terms of increasing suggestibility. As we shall see, many of our subjects have reported that the forty-eight-hour period is the toughest of S.D. Apparently in most cases if a man can get by that length of time he is good for at least another two days.

We now feel that we can devise a system that will enhance the increased suggestibility to an even greater extent. It is possible that the suggestions given by the experimenter will be much more effective if he is established as a figure of authority in the mind of the subject. Remember that in the data reported above the experimenter is merely an impersonal, practically unknown man to the subject. In effect the subject meets the experimenter, goes into S.D., and then sees him after S.D. Suggestibility probably can be increased if the subject is more dependent upon the experimenter *during* S.D.; for example, if the experimenter gives him his meals, permission to leave the bed to go to the toilet, tells him when he may sleep, interrupts his sleep with occasional tasks, regulates his water supply, and in general becomes part of his every activity, at the same time keeping his activities to a minimum.

It may also be possible to increase the influence of S.D. on suggestion by increasing the motivation to perform the given task well. For example, suppose we interrupt S.D. at various points to give the "suggested" part of the body-sway test, with the promise that if he performs well we will then release him from S.D. It seems logical that as the motivation to get out of S.D. increases he will become overanxious, tense, and very vulnerable to our suggestions.

We seem, once again, to have produced more questions than answers. However, we have found, by two different measures, that the suggestibility of man can be increased by S.D.

CHAPTER V

Does Man Have a Need for Stimulation?

WHEN food is withheld from an individual, he develops hunger. The same is true for water and air. It is also obvious that the longer the item is withheld the greater the need becomes. From this analogy it was an irresistible step to ask if withholding or greatly reducing stimulation in S.D. generated a need for it. More specifically, we came to ask if an individual would accept, or even seek, a form of stimulation in S.D. that would not normally interest him.

To get at this question, we placed within the cubicle a small box containing a viewing system that was the eyepiece of an old-fashioned stereoscope. On the box was a button that turned on a very dim light that illuminated the back inside wall of the viewing box. There the subject could see a simple black-on-white line drawing that consisted of two circles, one large, one small, and a slanting line between them. We tried to provide a neutral scene that would have as little intrinsic interest as possible.

The subject was given almost no instructions about the viewing box. Its position was indicated and its operation explained to each prior to his entry into S.D., and he was told nothing about the box except that it was there for his use and that he might use it as often as he pleased. The experimenters were able to note each time he used the viewing box, for the button that turned on the viewing light also activated a clock in the experimenter's area, and the light and the clock remained on as long as the subject held down the switch. We were thus able to determine when he looked into the viewer and the amount of time he spent doing so. We reasoned that, after the first couple of looks, if a man spent time at the viewer he was expressing a need for stimulation. I should point out that the level of illumination within the box was so low it could not be used for anything other than viewing the line drawings, and it was not possible for the subject to illuminate the cubicle or even to survey his hand held directly in front of the viewer.

The data, given in the table below, turned out to be more revealing than we had expected. Not only did we find a need for stimulation generated by S.D., but we also discovered that the utilization of the viewer clearly separated those subjects who demanded early release

Number of Subjects		Mean viewing time during first day of S.D.	Mean viewing time during total S.D.	Mean time in S.D.
Group I	6	183.2 sec.	212.5 sec.	37.6 hrs.
Group II	9	13.3	165.5	72

from those who did not. The findings came as a great surprise to us.

The six men in Group I all demanded an early release from S.D. Their average length of time of confinement was 37.6 hours, which again supports the belief that if one succeeds in getting past forty-eight hours of S.D. he will not push the panic button. The nine men in Group II all successfully completed their full term of seventy-two hours.

Note that the time spent at the viewer by Group I, during the first day of confinement, was significantly greater than that by Group II. These data seem to tell us two things: first, that the need for stimulation is generated early in S.D. for those subjects who are not adjusting well to it and who demand an early release; second, that little need for stimulation occurs in the initial phase of S.D. for those who successfully complete their confinement.

The unsuccessful group did not spend most of the first day sleeping. Instead, according to their reports, they had frequent fitful naps and attended to the viewing box during the awake period. The successful group paid little attention to the viewing box and spent most of the first day sleeping.

The need for stimulation seems to develop gradually even in the case of Group II; note that during the second and third days of confinement they spent enough time at the viewer to accumulate a total of 165.5 seconds. This particular finding met our expectations—

that the longer a man remained in S.D. the oftener he would look into the viewer, and that longer confinement would generate a greater need for diversion, the viewing box being almost the only form available.

Most of the subjects had ready explanations for their conduct with the viewer. Those who looked in it often claimed that they expected the scene to change. Those who looked in it infrequently said that they found it uninteresting and saw no reason to continue using it. It should be pointed out, however, in slight contrast to that claim, that no one looked in the viewer only *once*.

There was one man, however, who did not look in it at all, but he was playing a game with us. He was pretending to be a prisoner of war, something about which he had firsthand knowledge. He claimed that in a real prisoner-of-war situation, if his captors had told him of such a switch, the last thing he would ever do would be to use it. He would have suspected a booby trap or something of that nature. There can be little doubt that this kind of caution and alertness brought him safely through a very bad wartime situation, and it is of interest that S.D. brought back these old war memories with such force that he found it easy to imagine us as his captors.

All of our subjects expressed extreme disappointment with the viewing box. They had expected interesting material as well as possibly changing material. This suggests that we could have used this arrangement as a learning device; it is highly possible that we could have enticed our subjects into learning tasks they may not have done under any other circumstances. Suppose that one of our subjects had found some school subject, say, calculus, very distasteful. I believe that, despite such a dislike, he would be happy to spend time in S.D. studying calculus. I have no doubt that we could get him very excited about calculus while in S.D. merely by carefully programming the times it would be available to him. It would probably serve this end best to provide at random short study periods of about ten or so minutes each. The periods should be short in order to keep interest high, and they should not come frequently, thereby maintaining a need for stimulation. There is little doubt in my mind that we could arrange things so as to keep the attention of our subject focused constantly on the viewing box. More than this, he would be highly motivated to receive material from the viewing box, and with this motivation the speed of learning should be great.

One final comment about our subjects and the viewing box is of interest. Every now and again one of them reported seeing colors in the viewing box—yellow, orange, and red—though the drawings were black and white. These reports represent visual misinterpretations that are hard to explain, and at present we do not know the solution. It may be the beginning of a more serious phase of visual deterioration; it may indicate an overly imaginative attention by the viewer. In any case it is an item that deserves additional study.

Drs. Freedman, Grunebaum, and Grunblatt, of Harvard Medical School, have noted a related finding. Using confinement conditions very similar to those of the McGill studies, they found that subjects gave distorted descriptions of various kinds of figures after eight hours of confinement. The figures were: *a straight line* (all eight subjects saw it distorted), *a triangle* (two saw it distorted), *a cross* (two saw it distorted), and *three arrowheads* (seven saw them distorted). The distortions were in the form of movement and in changes in shape and size. None of these aberrations lasted longer than one hour after release from confinement.

Many of the S.D. studies report vivid visual effects occurring during confinement. These will be considered later in Part IV, Chapter XI.

CHAPTER VI

S.D. Orientation in Time

Our S.D. subjects, as mentioned earlier, showed a great deal of concern about time. They found it inconvenient and disturbing not to know the time. They felt an irresistible impulse to estimate the total time they had spent in S.D., and they incorrectly anticipated that we would ask them that question.

Obviously it is not only in S.D. that time becomes important, for man is normally very much concerned about it and controlled by it. Usually man is almost wholly dependent upon clocks for his knowledge of time. He actually pays little attention to time itself, but rather to the events that occur within a temporal frame of reference. Occasionally he does become aware of time itself, as when one is late for an appointment.

Many if not all organisms below man have some form of internal clock that helps to regulate their activities. For example, the honeybee "knows" the time of opening of certain flowers rich in nectar, so as to arrive on time. The homing pigeon holds a true course by reference to the sun, but, since the sun moves across the sky during the day, the pigeon must have some kind of internal clock that allows it to compensate for the sun's position. Certain shrimp, when disturbed, move out to sea and always by the shortest route; they determine the route by reference to the sun, which, as with the pigeon, must have its movement compensated by a clock. Birds and fish display a highly precise rhythm of migration. These activities occur almost precisely at the same time each year. Some arctic animals, such as the weasel, change the colors of their fur with the season. These are only a few of the examples of internal clocks in animals, most of which have been at least partially explained by science. In all explanations there is evidence pointing to some environmental factor that in turn controls some physiological factor. For example, consider that the migration of geese is a very precise thing. Study reveals that temperature and food supply are only secondary factors. The important factor is the *amount* of light or the length of day. The amount of light, it turns out, changes the size of the pituitary gland, often as much as five- or tenfold. The hormones secreted by this gland apparently serve as the mechanism that starts migrations, such as the journey north to their breeding grounds in the spring. To the reader who asks, "But why do they have their breeding grounds in the north?" I can only answer that he has captured the beginnings of the excitement of research. Imagine how great this excitement is when man is the subject of research.

If physiological changes can provide internal clocks for animals, is the same true for man? Such does not seem to be the case. Our ability to judge time without reference to clocks presents a unique problem. Most investigations of this ability have used short intervals. It has been found that intervals lasting less than a second are commonly *overestimated,* while intervals of more than a second are commonly *underestimated.* Estimates of longer intervals depend upon whether the interval is *filled* and upon the manner in which it is filled. Filled intervals are generally perceived as longer than unfilled intervals of the same objective length. For example, if an unfilled interval were marked off by two clicks, it would seem shorter than the same period filled with clicks. Even more important to our estimates of time is the nature of the material that fills the interval: the duration of the sound of a word is judged to be shorter than that of the sound of a noise lasting the same amount of time. A meaningful sentence is judged shorter than an equivalent series of nonsense syllables. In general it seems that factors that increase interest also decrease the perceived duration of time. This is the case, however, only when the temporal judgment is rendered during or immediately after the occurrence of the particular event. An event may seem intolerably drawn out, owing to its lack of interest, while it is going on, but in retrospect the interval shrinks almost to nothingness.

In the case of S.D. we naturally came to predict that judgment of temporal intervals would be overestimated, that the overestimates would be especially great, as S.D.

provided very empty, monotonous intervals of time. Our prediction, however, was wrong.

The question of time estimation during sensory deprivation was investigated by Drs. Choen, Silverman, Bressler, and Shmavonian, working at Duke University Medical Center. Their subjects were seated for four hours in a dark, soundproof chamber, and each of the four subjects was told to press a signal button when he estimated that thirty minutes had passed. Two of them pressed the signal prior to the thirty-minute interval, while the other two (judged to be of schizoid personalities) signaled after the thirty-minute period. In another study ten subjects were confined for two hours each under the same conditions. Nine of the subjects reported that they had been confined between a half hour and one and a half hours. As will be seen, this finding is in line with our results. One of their subjects grossly misjudged time and estimated that he had been confined for six hours.

TECHNIQUE FOR TESTING TIME ESTIMATES IN S.D.

After we placed a small button within easy reach of the S.D. subject, he was instructed to push the button at the end of what he estimated to be each hour of confinement. He was also instructed to estimate the amount of time spent sleeping. Each time he awoke he was to judge how many hours he had slept and so indicate by the number of pushes of the button, which was connected to a counter in the experimenter's area so that the subject's estimates could be compared against elapsed clock time. A sample record will serve to explain this procedure.

Counter Number	Actual Clock Time	Actual Elapsed Time	
		HOURS	MINUTES
0	10:28 A.M.		
1	11:30	1	2
2–3	1:21 P.M.	1	51
4	2:44	1	23
5	5:45	3	1
6	7:12	1	27
7	8:15	1	3
8	9:03		48
9	10:39	1	36
10	2:48 A.M.	4	9
11	5:16	2	28
12	7:25	2	9
13	9:07	1	42
14	10:39	1	32

(At 10:28 A.M. the first day of S.D. was completed.)

This subject entered S.D. at 10:28 A.M. and first pushed the button at 11:30 A.M., indicating that one hour had passed. Actually this particular estimate was very accurate, and this seldom occurred with other subjects. As the record proceeds, however, until the end of the first twenty-four hours of S.D. our subject indicated the passage of only fourteen hours, underestimating the first day by ten hours. In this time he had also estimated that he slept only two hours, as indicated by the Counter Numbers 2 and 3 occurring together. Remember that each number on the counter stands for one hour in the mind of the subject. The actual elapsed time for each estimated hour can be seen in the last column on the right.

In the manner described we confined six subjects for ninety-six hours. Figure 1 indicates the results.

The data above are the accumulated estimates of each subject. If the data for a given subject had been indicated by a straight horizontal line, it would have meant that he had estimated time accurately. If the line had slanted upward, it would have meant that he was overestimating the time interval, as we had predicted he would. The data, however, show very clearly that our prediction was wrong and that S.D. subjects *underestimated* time intervals.

Note that three of our subjects (1, 2, and 3) were the heavy losers. They accumulated the greatest loss of time by underestimating the hourly interval. Subject 1 indicated only fifty-seven hours instead of ninety-six, while Subjects 2 and 3 indicated only sixty-seven hours. In other words, these men had lost thirty-nine and twenty-nine hours, respectively, out of four days.

Subjects 4, 5, and 6 also resemble each other and are vastly different from the first three. Though Subject 6 will be discussed separately, this group is distinct from the first because of its greater accuracy of time

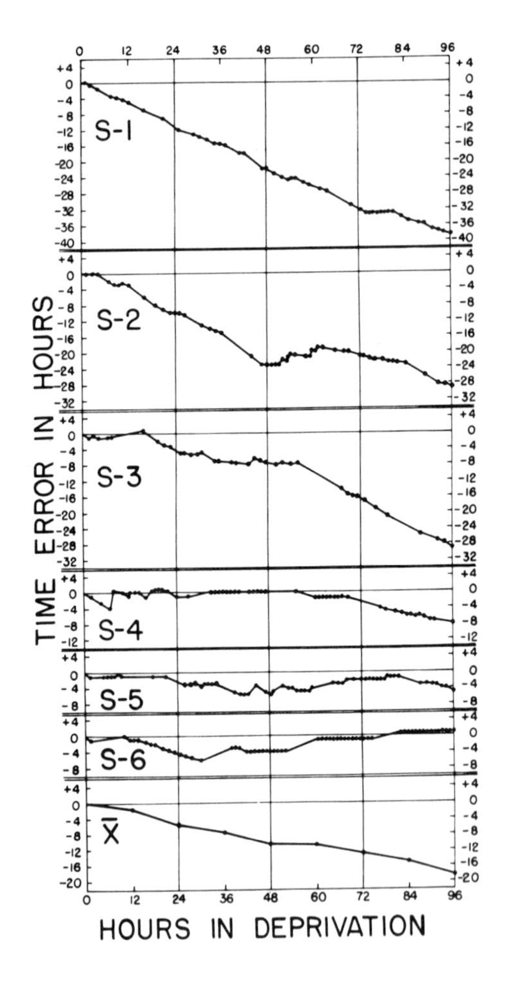

FIG. 1.

estimates, which were so good that by the end of four days Subject 4 had lost only eight hours, and Subject 4 had lost only four hours, while Subject 6 was within one half an hour.

The first three subjects not only grossly underestimated elapsed time, they also did a poor job of estimating the time spent in sleep. None of them ever indicated sleeping more than *three hours* at a time. This is quite different from our expected eight hours of sleep per night. When we questioned them on this point, each answered that he planned to sleep in short tours as a method of breaking up S.D.

The second group of subjects used as many things they could think of to aid in their estimates. They paid attention to the rate of cooling of the soup in the food chest, growth of beard, the rate of drying out of the washrag placed by the chemical toilet, how their eyes felt upon awaking from sleep, as well as the accumulation of matter at the corners of the eyes, so that their estimates of sleeping time were very good. They thought about time, about how long various mental activities required, they frequently "checked" a short period of time, such as five minutes, by counting it off. They tried to check long intervals of time against hunger pangs and the rate of urine generation.

When the record for Subject 6 is considered, one can well imagine that we suspected he had a clock in S.D. by which to control his estimates. In a sense he did have a clock—one he had invented. After we instructed him to give us his best estimates of time, he took us very seriously, in fact too much so. He spent the early part of his confinement trying to think up some method by which he could tell time. On the graph above note that during the first day and a half of S.D. he was underestimating the hourly elapse of time, but during that period he was inventing his clock.

He started by asking himself if there were something that recurred regularly that he could use to denote the passage of time. He soon hit upon the idea that his own pulse would fit his needs. Here he ran into a problem, for he did not know that the average normal adult heart rate is around sixty-seven to seventy-two beats per minute. (This rate, incidentally, probably would be slower in S.D.) Without this knowledge our subject was faced with the problem of determining how much time his pulse required. The presence of an apple in the food chest suggested a pendulum, and by using it he measured his pulse. On the wall of the chamber he tore loose some flexible hookup wire (fortunately it was abandoned wire and not that leading to the experimenter's counter). In the manner of a seamstress measuring material he estimated a yard of wire, which he tied to the apple and thus hung a pendulum, and, applying Newton's second law of motion, he was able to calculate the period of the pendulum. With this method he then determined that his heart rate was ninety beats per minute. Such a small error can be easily forgiven because he had to solve the equation in the dark, feeling the movement of the pendulum and approximating the length of the pendulum and the weight of the apple.

After measuring his pulse rate he easily calculated

that 5400 heartbeats represented one hour. All he then had to do was to count off the appropriate number of beats and push the button accordingly. In this manner he began the amazingly accurate determination that can be seen after one and a half days of his record in the graph above. He had not counted off many hours before he found it inconvenient to keep track of such large numbers, so he devised a tally recorder. He removed ten nails from the soft beaverboard strips lining the room. He then stuck these nails back into the beaverboard, forming a double horizontal row of nails with five nails in each section. All of this he could accomplish without leaving the bed.

Hundreds	Thousands
0 0 0 0 0	0 0 0 0 0
0 0 0 0 0	0 0 0 0 0

The first bank of nails was the hundreds counters and the second was the thousands counters. With this he never had to count higher than one hundred heartbeats at one time. Each time he counted a hundred he removed a nail from the first bank and moved it down one row until he had moved all five nails. He then systematically moved each nail back to its original position so that when all the hundreds counters were back in their original position he had counted off one thousand beats, and he indicated this by moving down one row the first nail of the thousands counter. He proceeded in this fashion until he had all five of the nails in the thousands counter moved down plus four of the nails in the hundreds counter, which would total 5400, or the time to signal the passage of one hour. As can be seen in the graph his "clock" was almost perfect.

In the later stages of S.D. he tried other schemes for counting, such as combining pulse beats so that three beats equaled four seconds. He always returned to his original plan, however, because he felt that any other device interrupted his thoughts. It seems that counting his pulse became so automatic he could engage in other thoughts at the same time. I find this a truly amazing feat of mental gymnastics, but he complained that he was unable to do as much serious thinking in S.D. as he had planned.

This one subject serves very well to illustrate how resourceful some people can become when placed under a condition of demand. In fact it is probably the case that all humans become more ingenious when put to the test. Sensory deprivation became for this subject a challenge, and there can be no doubt that he more than met it.

THE ESTIMATE OF SHORT TIME INTERVALS

We also wanted to know how these same subjects would estimate short intervals of time as well as longer intervals. Thus we asked that when they pushed the button to signal the lapse of one hour they hold the button in for *five seconds*. The button was wired into the circuit of an electric clock so that its action started and stopped the clock, and in this fashion we were able to get many measures of how well subjects could estimate five seconds. We were unable to get this estimate from Subject 2, owing to his failure to understand the instruction. He thought that he was to make only one such estimate and on the first hour only.

The table below presents the average estimate by each subject of the five-second interval, and his record of the total time he lost in his designations of elapsed hours.

Subject Number	Average Estimate of Five Seconds	Total Loss by Hourly Designations
1	3.3	38
3	4.5	29
4	6.5	8
5	7.2	4
6	6.0	-½

Several things are of interest here. First, each subject was so constant in his short estimates as to be significantly different from the others. Second, there is the possibility of a relationship between the two types of interval estimates: it appears that the greater the accumulated underestimate of the hourly period, the greater the underestimate of the five-second interval. The data above conform perfectly to this thought, but obviously there are far too few subjects to permit a serious conclusion. Such information may be of vital importance to astronauts, who would probably have to make many time estimates in the event of instrument failure. It becomes an important question as to whether one can be trained to improve the capacity to estimate time elapse. Could we have trained those subjects so that their estimates were more accurate? There is little doubt that it would be possible to produce high accuracy in this ability of man.

It is hard to say what causes man to underestimate time under the conditions of S.D. We are able, however, to state one thing that does *not* cause it. Our subjects were not deliberately underestimating time so as to protect themselves. Each man insisted that he gave estimates to the very best of his ability, without any consideration other than being as accurate as possible. At this point we are left with the conclusion that under conditions such as those in S.D. man be expected to underestimate time intervals of the durations considered above.

One final comment about these subjects. They were confined for ninety-six hours, and not one pushed the panic button or even considered demanding an early release. From our other studies in S.D. we had expected that one or two of these men would request release. Again, we need more data, but the obvious suggestion is irresistible, namely, that any task performed during S.D. renders this confinement more tolerable, that under such stark conditions one finds it desirable to do something, even an act as simple as pushing a button once an hour.

PART THREE

Sensory Deprivation and Its Effect Upon Learning

CHAPTER VII

Can One Think during S.D.?

MANY people, when first confronted with the idea of S.D., predict that it would surely drive them crazy. They are, of course, overstating the case, but there is no question that S.D. directly involves mental capacity. It is more than speculation that in some circumstances S.D. can adversely affect the intellect.

That people should expect to be so influenced by S.D. is not surprising. It is perhaps more surprising that we were able to get people to serve as subjects in such an experiment. The fact that we paid them twenty dollars per day was some inducement, but it was probably not enough in itself. Our subjects came to us for a variety of reasons. To be sure, the pay was important to them, but they also had a great deal of curiosity about the project, about themselves, and they expected to find it conducive to concentration. Since nearly all of the S.D. subjects were graduate students, they came to us with a sizable backlog of intellectual problems that they planned to work on during S.D. Since some of our first subjects reported that they could not think during S.D., we came to ask each about his thinking process during confinement. The McGill studies found that concentration became too difficult after a period of sensory deprivation. The Goldberger and Holt study, mentioned in Chapter I, found that there was a loss of continuity of thought accompanying S.D. In another study, by Mendelson, Kubzansky, Leiderman, Wexler, and Solomon, of the Department of Psychiatry, Harvard Medical School, the same result was reported despite the use of entirely different conditions of confinement. Subjects were placed in a tank-type respirator so that restriction of movement was great, and there was a great deal of sensory stimulation, as the room containing the respirator was lighted and not sound-shielded. A screen was placed about the respirator so that the subject looked at blank white walls.

In normal life our thinking process is a fairly active, almost constantly ongoing process. It can engage in a great variety of activities, ranging from the mere free associations about stimuli to the height of purely creative activity. Probably the vast majority of what we call thinking is our reactions to daily stimulation. We "think" about those things we read, see, and hear. In other words, much of our thinking is dependent upon things and other people. It is also paradoxically true that things and other people can serve as distractions that effectively prevent the more creative type of thinking. Thus it is easy to see why our subjects concluded that S.D. would provide a period of productive thinking.

There are those who believe that, regardless of the kind of thought that is going on, the brain must be constantly bombarded by outside stimuli to be capable of thinking. They feel that nerve impulses must be fed into the brain from the various sense departments in order to keep the brain active and alert. This process can go too far. If the system is overloaded by too much stimulation, man may become incapable of concentration. Between these two extremes, so goes this reasonable hypothesis, man lives out most of his life.

In S.D. we have a situation that probably leads to a reduction of brain bombardment, as there is a marked reduction in sensory stimulation. Obviously all stimulation did not cease for our S.D. subjects; but the question is: Did enough remain to permit and/or improve thought?

By far the vast majority of our subjects said that the first day of S.D. was an excellent period for concentration; that is, those parts of the first day not spent in sleeping. They reported that they felt their powers of concentration were better than usual, that thoughts were easily confined to a single subject matter, that their efforts to think were slight and the production very clear and precise. They referred to it as a period of sharpened thought. That S.D. provided an absence of distraction as well as restful sleep makes these claims very plausible. The kinds of things about which our subjects thought were as varied as the backgrounds of the subjects themselves. In some cases they went along thinking about and working on the problems associated with their studies. One subject claimed that he felt he had a deeper and clearer penetration into certain aspects of theoretical physics. He felt that he was able to ask various questions about the subject matter which were of better quality than any of his previous attempts. When his instructors were informed of his questions, some of them confirmed his evaluation.

Not all S.D. subjects worked on school matters. Some used S.D. to work on those things for which they usually did not have time. One subject composed a song, music and lyrics, as an anniversary present for his wife. He was very pleased with his production, claiming that it was far superior to any of his previous attempts. Another subject perfected and extended a "memory feat." Prior to S.D. this man reported that he was able to recite any list of items up to thirty in number after hearing the list only one time. During S.D. he worked on this feat until he could recall up to a hundred items. Though he needed still more time to practice his skill, even a crude check proved his claim.

These are some examples of better mental production of people in S.D., but not all were so fortunate. Even some who did well during the first day found later confinement to be a different matter. Everything considered, fully one half of our subjects complained of difficulty in thinking. The typical complaint was simply that they could not maintain thought. They would initiate an idea on which they wished to work, only to have it evaporate almost as quickly as they initiated it. They were unable to keep a thought process going along a particular subject. It was as though they had lost disciplinary control over the thinking process. It was not a loss of control that frightened them or caused them to believe that they were, say, going out of their minds, but they did find it undesirable and disappointing, as well as mildly unpleasant. When they were asked what they did when their thinking process more or less "got out of control," to a man they replied that they engaged in excessive daydreaming. They seemed to be fairly passive to the process and content merely to attend to whatever daydreams happened to occur—they were unable to determine the nature of them.

There were some subjects who represented yet a third kind of thought process during S.D. They could think, they could control the nature and direction of their thoughts up to a point, they could maintain thought, but their thoughts became irritatingly and compellingly repetitious. One subject made up a game of listing, according to the alphabet, each chemical reaction that bore the name of the discoverer. At the letter *n* he was unable to think of an example. He tried to skip *n* and go on, but *n* kept doggedly coming up in his mind, demanding an answer. When this became tiresome, he tried to dismiss the game altogether, only to find that he could not. He endured the insistent demand of his game for a short time, and, finding that he was unable to control it, he pushed the panic button.

Another subject amused himself by doing the multiplication table, a game that went very well until he got into the high end of thirteen. Stumped at first, he started again, did the table once more, and came to a halt at the same place for the second time. He then tried to start the game for the third try, only to discover that he was repeatedly asking himself, "What is thirteen times eleven?" or "What is thirteen times twelve?" These thoughts had so much force and became so compelling that he too pushed the panic button.

Not all of those who invented mental games to help pass the time in S.D. were unsuccessful. One successful effort that occurred often was the learning of the alphabet backward, a game that had the advantage of novelty, was difficult enough to be engrossing, and did not cause defeat. When a subject got lost, he could recover himself by saying the alphabet forward up to the point of difficulty.

It was desirable, for maximum distraction, that the game not end too quickly, but also that it not go on indefinitely. Ideal was a game that required repetition and did not overwhelm the subject.

In summary, then, the effects of S.D. upon the thinking process are varied. For a few, thinking continues to be very clear and perhaps even better than normally. For most, however, the conditions of S.D. seem almost cruelly calculated to produce difficulties in the thinking process, typically a subject who entered S.D. anticipating a period of productive thought and who brought with him many problems to think about. At first he thought very well, had good penetration and keen insights, but this period was short-lived, and usually by the second day he found that a drastic change had occurred. Not only were his thoughts muddled, but he was usually unable to maintain any particular thought, and at this point he would either push the panic button and leave S.D. or complete it by allowing daydreams to pass in an uninterrupted sequence.

Those who lost their ability to concentrate, about two out of three subjects, usually refused to admit it. They made excuses for their failures which placed the blame away from themselves, often claiming that they were capable of thinking but that it seemed pointless in the absence of anyone with whom to discuss their thoughts. Others insisted that for the first time they realized how important a paper and pencil were to their thinking process. One subject insisted that he was unable to think because he was not permitted to talk out loud.

When questioned, all subjects reported that their thinking process would have been better if some other person had been available. Most of them felt that the presence of a listener provided a justification for their thinking. Only occasionally did we encounter the rare individual who was so confident about his thinking process as not to need the minor assurances of another person.

Since most subjects tended to place great importance upon the need of a "listener," would it have been possible to fool them? Could we have indicated that a listener was constantly at the other end of a microphone and thereby have maintained relatively good thinking for all subjects? I have no doubt that such a scheme would have worked. I am confident that S.D. subjects would be satisfied if they *believed* they had an audience.

These findings tend to stress, it would appear, the importance that social interaction has for all of us. For most of our subjects S.D. was probably the first extended asocial experience of their lives. This, added to the other conditions of S.D., produced a situation where a person may very well come to doubt the need for productive activity of any sort—mental or otherwise. One certainly cannot think in an intellectual vacuum, a condition produced in high degree by sensory deprivation.

It is now possible with these findings to make certain recommendations. If it were desirable to train people to endure confinement better, we would suggest: (a) maintain the thinking process by employing simple "games," (b) improve the powers of concentration by repetition of thoughts, (c) minimize frustration by providing "checks" for the thinking process, (d) increase the motivation to control thinking by pretending to have an audience or a listener to whom the material of the thoughts is directed, (e) avoid the easy habit of drifting with the ever-present and ever-ready day-dreaming or fantasy, and (f) avoid fatigue by deliberately introducing an occasional brief period of day-dreaming.

CHAPTER VIII

The Effects of S.D. upon Learning

EARLIER studies conducted at McGill University found that confinement produced some form of intellectual deterioration. Our studies, as indicated in Chapter VII, have produced similar findings. Thus it was natural that we should come to ask what effect S.D. would have on the learning process. Since the thinking process suffers because of S.D., we expected to find a similar decrement in the learning process, and we proceeded to measure it in the following way.

A very simple learning task was selected, assuming that subsequent studies would use more difficult material. The task selected was the simple learning by rote of a list of *eight* words—a list such as: "noonday, boastful, exact, perfect, awkward, crafty, lawful, famous." The subject worked at learning the list by the method of anticipation—each word became the cue for the next word. Ever-repeating lists of the words were placed on a tape recorder. The subject listened to the first play-through of the list, and at the end of it he tried to anticipate the first word on the list before the tape recorder played it. Shortly after his anticipation the tape recorder presented the word. In this manner he could check his response and then go on to anticipate the next word, and so on through the list. Each word was separated on the tape by two seconds so that the subject had time to make his anticipation of the word before it was played, but not enough time to practice between words. An experimenter recorded all the responses made by the subject.

The task was considered complete when the subject produced the entire list without error. The speed of learning was measured by the number of times the list had to be repeated before the subject was successful. The first learning task was given to him before he entered S.D. This performance served as a basis of comparison for later tests and was considered to be a measure of his normal learning rate for such tests.

Without previous notification S.D. was interrupted at the end of twenty-four hours for the second learning test, which consisted of eight *different* words of comparable difficulty. Since the subject called out his anticipations, and since the tape recorder played the material, there was no need for vision in order to perform the task. Thus all tests were conducted in the dark in the cubicle by microphone and speaker.

In a similar manner a third learning task was given in the cubicle after forty-eight hours of S.D., and the subject was then released from confinement. At the end of the twenty-four hours after his release from S.D. he was called back to the laboratory for another test, and two days later was called back for the final test. Thus the schedule provided for one test before confinement, two tests during, and two tests after.

In order to evaluate properly the accumulated data, we needed a control group, and after forming one we ran it through the *same* tests, conducted in the *same* manner, as those for the S.D. subjects. The control subjects also took their tests in the S.D. cubicle, but were released at the end of each test. The need for such "controls" was obvious, for without control data we would not have known whether any improvement in learning was due to S.D. or merely to practice. Figure 2 presents the average performance of each group for each test. There were four subjects each in the control and the S.D. group, and the data in the chart are the average performances for each group.

To begin with, note that Test 1 indicates that the two groups are very similar in their ability to learn. At Test 2 the control group has retained its ability and shows almost no change from the measurement at Test 1. The S.D. group, which has been in twenty-four hours of S.D., shows a significant change. It has improved its learning ability considerably, learning the task in fourteen trials, as compared to twenty for the control group. At Test 3 the S.D. group continued to improve, reaching the level of learning the list in only eight trials, whereas the control group required twenty-six trials for the same task. For the control this represents a deterioration of performance which is hard to explain unless one assumes that Test 3 was more dif-

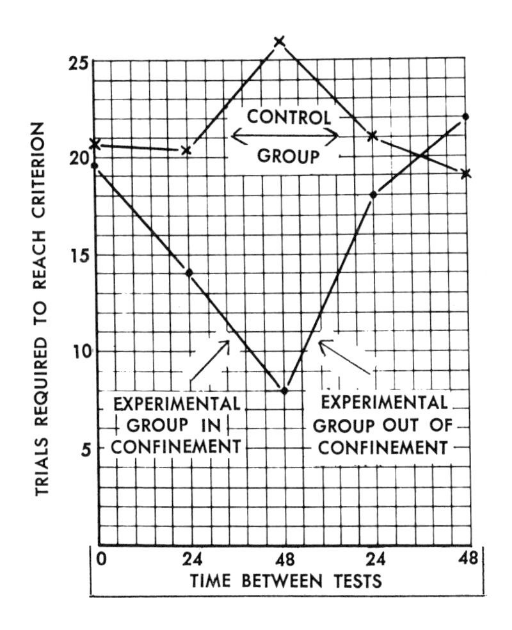

FIG. 2. EFFECT OF S.D. UPON A SIMPLE LEARNING TASK.

ficult than the others. The important thing, nevertheless, is that S.D. brought about a significant increase in learning ability.

Test 4 shows the S.D. group returning to normal performance levels, for at this test they have been out of S.D. for twenty-four hours. One may conclude that the increase in performance that occurs in S.D. does not persist very long after it. Note that at Test 5 the S.D. group, now out of confinement for forty-eight hours, is slightly but not significantly worse than the control group.

The conclusions of these data are obvious: S.D. produced an increase in the speed of learning where the learning task was a simple one. As the confinement continued, up to forty-eight hours, so did improvement, but it did not persist for long after release and was almost entirely gone twenty-four hours afterward.

These data were clearly not the expected results, for we had expected the learning process to deteriorate much as the thinking process had. However, there may be a vast difference in the two processes during S.D. It seems reasonable to state that if one cannot concentrate, ordinarily he will do a poor job of thinking; and that in S.D. the individual was unable to concentrate, possibly because he had to depend upon self-initiated situations, whereas with the learning task the solitude was broken by the tape recorder. Perhaps he could concentrate upon this because it came as such a contrast to his other S.D. experiences. It may suggest that he was so highly motivated to receive any form of stimulation that even a learning task was a welcome one. Conclusions, however, must be reserved until after the next study, where similar findings did not occur.

S.D. AND MORE DIFFICULT LEARNING TASKS

After the results of the previous study it was impossible not to ask the question "If forty-eight hours of S.D. can improve learning ability so much, will not seventy-two hours do even more?" Unfortunately we cannot answer that question for the simple reason that we became overly ambitious in the next study and obfuscated the data by trying to do too much. The mistake we made was to ask: "What will happen to the S.D. effect on learning if the task is made more difficult?"

Once again we used the method of anticipation, but for a more difficult task. Each subject was required to learn lists of fifteen words each instead of eight as before. The schedule of tests was so arranged that after the first twenty-four hours they were given every twelve hours during S.D. The testing schedule was as follows:

Test Number	When Given
1	before confinement
2	after 24 hours of confinement
3	after 36
4	after 48
5	after 60
6	after 72
7	24 hours after release
8	36 hours after
9	48 hours after

The same schedule of testing was administered to a control group, and all conditions were the same for the two groups except that the control subjects remained in the S.D. cubicle only long enough to take the test at each test period. None of the subjects was informed as to the schedule of tests or that there would ever be additional tests. There were nine subjects in each group.

According to the previous test, it was expected that the S.D. subjects would continue to improve in their learning ability, at least up to forty-eight hours of confinement and perhaps even beyond. Such was not the case. In the beginning the S.D. group tended to show a slight improvement over the comparable control group, but it was not a significant difference. In fact there was *no significant difference* between the two groups throughout the entire testing schedule. This finding seems to indicate clearly that the advantage for learning that we found previously holds for only simple tasks, for in the second study we made the task more difficult and lost the advantage even though we increased the amount of S.D. Taken together, these findings suggest that for even more difficult material S.D. might produce a deterioration effect. But before considering the case of even more difficult learning material, let me say that we are far from finished with the data of the above study using the fifteen-word lists. As it turned out, those data required a special analysis to separate the S.D. and control groups. The analysis and its result will be taken up in the next chapter.

To test the effects of S.D. on even more complex tasks, we used a problem-solving task. Though an individual problem can be very complex, it has the disadvantage that once one problem has been successfully solved there is high positive transfer to many other problems, making them easier to solve. It is therefore more difficult to have problems of equal difficulty than to have equally difficult word lists. Because of this consideration we tested only once the ability to solve problems, and that at the end of seventy-two hours of S.D.

We used the technique of *concept formation,* which requires that the subject solve a series of problems. The technique can best be illustrated by a simplified example: The tester presents a red square, a green triangle, and a yellow circle all in a row and asks, "Which is correct?" If the subject replied, "The yellow circle," and the tester says, "Correct," does the subject know why his answer is correct? No, he knows only that there are several *possible* concepts that make it correct and that by continued trials he must get the proper one. He knows that his answer was correct for one of the following reasons: (1) because it was a circle, (2) because it was yellow, (3) because it was the figure just to the right of the triangle, (4) because it was the figure just to the right of the color green, (5) because it was the figure twice removed from the square, (6) because it was the figure twice removed from the color red, (7) because it was the figure to the extreme right, and so on. Thus suppose that the second presentation is: yellow square, green circle, and red triangle (the concept governing correctness is the same as above). Which is correct for the second presentation? If the correct response for this presentation is the red triangle, how many of the above concepts generated by the first presentation now hold?* In this manner the presentations are continued until the subject can state the *exact single concept* that governs the correctness and incorrectness of responses. The subject is allowed only one "vote" per presentation. In this case the correct concept was always the figure on the extreme right.

The concept-formation problem actually used was much more difficult, for it had sixteen items, each of which had four different dimensions, and the subjects had to discover the *one concept* that determined the sorting of the items into four piles of four each. If the reader is mystified by the concept problem, it is understandable, but it is enough here for him to know that a very difficult problem was given to the subjects.

The data were very clear-cut. The S.D. subjects were significantly *worse* than the control subjects. Both groups by other measures were equal in their learning ability, yet after seventy-two hours of confinement the S.D. group was very poor at concept formation. Two of the nine S.D. subjects were unable to solve the problem at all, and another required one hundred trials to get it. The average performance of the S.D. group, discounting the two who could not solve it at all, was forty-one trials to get the correct solution. The control group required an average of only ten trials. Apparently most S.D. subjects had the same difficulty with their solutions. They were unable to dismiss the

*This solution could be true according to Concepts 4, 5, or 7.

first attempted solution in order to attempt another and different one. The old solution kept "popping into mind" even though it had proved to be inadequate. The control subjects frequently also reported the persistence of some discarded solution, but only when they were momentarily stuck for a new attempt.

In summary, then, we found that S.D. was beneficial for the learning of simple tasks, that it had no effect upon more complex tasks, and that it had a deleterious effect upon very complex problem solving.

These data suggest that, even with its advantageous lack of distractions, S.D. is not the desirable set of conditions for serious learning. For this other procedures should be tried. I am convinced that by properly arranging S.D. learning could be greatly facilitated, but that only additional research will provide the answer. It may be necessary to interrupt confinement so that the subject is confined for, say, twenty-four or thirty-six hours. At the end of that time, while still in S.D., the lights come on and he is instructed to study a given subject for an hour, at the end of which he goes back into darkened S.D., and his retention of the studied material is measured a day or two later upon the release from S.D. By waiting until after a day or so of S.D. has passed he should be highly motivated to study anything, if only to break the monotony. Then going back into S.D. would provide time in which he could think about and review the material he had studied. I predict that he would have a greater retention of that material.

CHAPTER IX

Some Subtle Effects of S.D. upon Difficult Learning

FROM the work discussed in the previous chapter we had concluded that S.D. had a facilitating effect on learning when the learning task was simple, and that this effect disappeared when the task became difficult. We found the absence of effect hard to understand or even to believe, so we continued our studies. We decided that S.D. had been interrupted too many times for meals, toilet calls, and testing periods, even though these had been made to coincide whenever possible. Our next studies were conducted without these interruptions. The food was placed in the chamber so that the subject fed himself, but in the dark, to be sure. We also placed relief bottles in the confinement cell and a chemical toilet in the antechamber. Thus the subjects had no occasion to leave the S.D. room at any time. We reasoned that the new procedure provided a more severe form of S.D. and should therefore yield effects either to a greater extent or more quickly.

We used twenty-four subjects who were first divided into two groups of twelve subjects each. The two were matched as to their learning ability for roto memory tasks; the mean performance on a pretest for one group was thirty trials and for the other it was twenty-eight. One group became the subjects and the other became the control group. Each group was divided into three subgroups of four each. Once again the members were matched as to their learning ability for rote memory according to their pretest performances.

Each subject received two tests of his learning ability, one just before he entered confinement and another just after his release. Each control subject also received two tests, separated by the same time spent in confinement by those in his comparison S.D. subgroups, each of which was confined for a different length of time. The three S.D. subgroups spent twenty-four, forty-eight, and seventy-two hours, respectively, in confinement. The comparable control subgroups spent the same periods of time between the first and second tests. Naturally the control subjects were out in the normal world between their tests while the S.D. subjects were in confinement, although *all* subjects were tested as before under identical conditions within the cubicle.

When each subject had finished taking his first test, he was given no indication that he would have to take another. We did not want him to practice learning of any sort between tests and thus render a better second performance.

The difference between the two performances was taken as an indication of the effect of what occurred in the time between the two tests. Figures 3 and 4 present these results.

Figure 3 shows, first, that each subject improved on the second performance (the two tests were matched as to their level of difficulty). It shows that the amount of improvement depends upon the amount of time between the tests and that the *direction* of the trend of improvement depends upon the ways the interval was filled. Note that, if the interval was spent in S.D., increasing the time produced less and less improvement. The S.D. subgroup confined for twenty-four hours improved, on the average, twelve trials, while the forty-eight-hour S.D. group improved an average of slightly fewer than six trials, and the seventy-two-hour S.D. group improved only slightly over one trial. The control subjects also improved in their performance, but the trend was opposite that of the S.D. subjects, that is, toward *more* improvement as the time between tests increased. In referring again to Figures 3 and 4, note that the control subgroups of twenty-four, forty-eight, and seventy-two hours improved three, seven, and nine trials, respectively.

The graph seems to say two things: that the beneficial effects of S.D. upon rote learning decrease as S.D. continues; that without S.D. there should have been a progressive increase in the learning ability. When S.D. was as long as seventy-two hours, there was no improvement, which suggests that longer confinements would produce a decrement.

FIG. 3.
S.D. SUBJECTS

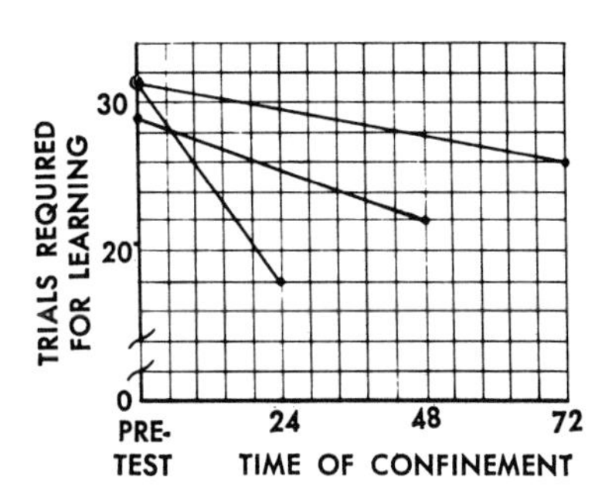

Note that all three groups start out in the pre-confinement test very close together. The second learning test after various periods of confinement shows an increase in learning ability or a reduction in number of trials required to learn. But how much of this improvement is due to "learning-how-to-learn" and would have occurred on the second learning task without confinement being imposed between the two tasks? The data for the control group below answer that question.

FIG. 4.
CONTROL SUBJECTS

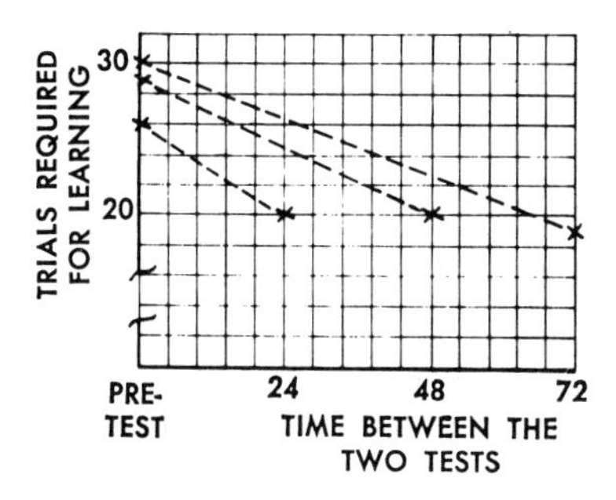

Note that the control subjects also improve; in fact, for 48 and 72 hours they improve more than the confined subjects.

Each subject was given a third, final test, which for the S.D. group came twenty-four hours after release, and for the control group twenty-four hours after the second test. The results of the third test show all subjects to be very much alike. Everyone, S.D. and control subjects alike, gained about ten trials over his first performance. This finding suggests that the effects rendered in S.D. do not carry over into postconfinement life.

HOW MANY KINDS OF ERRORS WERE MADE?

In the study just cited we found a rather striking difference between the performance of those in S.D. and that of the control group. Yet previously, as noted in Chapter VIII, we had found no difference between S.D. and control groups when difficult learning tasks were employed. This made us suspect that perhaps there were differences in the data which we had failed to detect, and that was precisely the case. In fact quite a bit of information had escaped our detection. The first thing we found was the manner in which our subjects had made their errors. They were credited with an error if they failed to make any response at all or if they made one that was incorrect. We called incorrect responses *overt errors*. When we counted we found that the S.D. group made significantly fewer overt errors than the control group, but before and after confinement the S.D. group made as many overt errors as its counterpart. It follows, considering the total number of errors, that during S.D. the confined group made significantly more errors of omission than did the control group. Thus the difference between the performances of these two groups was not the number of trials needed to learn the task, but the manner in which they achieved the learning. It is possible that our S.D. subjects were influenced by the instructions to remain quiet in confinement, though of course it was obvious that they had to break silence in order to take the test.

FLUCTUATION CYCLES

The term "fluctuation cycle" has special meaning in the psychological literature dealing with learning. Dr. Clark Hull, the psychologist already mentioned, was the first to use the term. He applied it to a special case of forgetting which occurs while one is in the process of some learning task. Take the case of our subjects who had to learn a list of fifteen words to the point of being able to repeat in correct order the entire list without error. In such situations it often happens that a particular word is given correctly at one time, only to be forgotten at some later time. A fluctuation cycle is said to have occurred when an incorrect response is both preceded and followed by a correct one. The somewhat schematic table below will help explain fluctuation cycles.

Word Number	Trials					
	1	2	3	4	5	6
1	x	v	ⓧ	v	v	v
2	x	x	v	ⓧ	v	v
3	x	v	v	v	ⓧ	v
4	v	v	ⓧ	ⓧ	ⓧ	v
And so on to 15	x	x	v	v	v	v

v = correct responses
x = incorrect responses

The circled *x*'s are examples of fluctuation cycles. Note what happened to the first word on the list. Our hypothetical subject missed it on the first trial, got it correct on the second trial, only to miss it on the third trial, but thereafter got it correct. Thus on the third trial he had a fluctuation cycle for the first word because he had previously gotten it correct and after an error he subsequently got it correct. In a similar fashion Word 2 has a fluctuation cycle on Trial 4, and Word 3 on Trial 5. Note the special case for Word 4. The three misses at Trials 3, 4, and 5 count for only *one* fluctuation cycle.

When we counted the fluctuation cycles in the learning performances, we found the following: Before and after confinement the S.D. subjects made the *same number* of cycles as did the control group, but during confinement the S.D. group made significantly *fewer*.

Clark Hull claimed that the fluctuation cycle was

caused by a form of forgetting. He judged the correct response just prior to the fluctuation cycle to be a case of learning that had reached a *very low level* and hence easily forgotten or, more correctly stated, easily interfered with so as to be forgotten. It would appear that our S.D. subjects did not forget so easily as did control subjects. When we consider the nature of forgetting, these findings seem to be reasonable. The best evidence to date shows that we forget things because other, and similar, things come along to create an interference. Obviously, when a thing is not well learned, interference can be more easily produced. It is also obvious that while the sources of interference are many they all stem from activities that are greatly reduced in S.D. Thus it seems proper that learning performances during S.D. should display a reduced number of fluctuation cycles because there was less opportunity for interference.

The idea of increased retention of newly learned material during the S.D. experience was demonstrated in another way. Twenty subjects were confined for twenty-four hours in the usual manner. Immediately upon being placed in the chamber they were instructed to listen carefully to a passage to be read to them. They were also instructed to be prepared to repeat as much as possible of the passage when it ended. This was their immediate recall test. At the end of twenty-four hours they were asked to repeat the passage just prior to release.

Control subjects were treated in exactly the same manner, except, of course, they were released during the twenty-four-hour period. They always performed worse on the second recall test than upon the immediate recall test, that is, they experienced a significant amount of forgetting over the twenty-four-hour period.

In contrast to this finding the S.D. subjects were as good at the second recall as at the immediate recall; they did not forget the material during the twenty-four hours of S.D.

These findings are very much in line with the previous one concerning the fluctuation cycles. The conditions of S.D. are such as to offer very little interference to learned material; hence little forgetting occurs during S.D.

EFFICIENCY OF LEARNING

Once we got the idea of analyzing our data at the level of the individual response, we came to ask another question, one related to the fluctuation cycle measures and the efficiency of our subjects' responses. Efficiency was defined as the difference between the number of trials required to make one errorless repetition of the list and the number of trials required to get each word on the list correct at least once. In this hypothetical example, suppose that by the twentieth trial our subject has at one time or another gotten each word on the list correct at least once, but it takes him forty trials in order to give all the words correctly on a single trial. His inefficiency ratio would be $40-20 \div 40 = .50$, or 50 per cent. The lower the ratio the better the performance.

In the case of our learning data we found that prior to confinement our control and S.D. subjects were nearly equally efficient: the control group's ratio was .62, while that of the S.D. group was .56. The slight difference favoring the S.D. group (6 per cent) is so small in this case as to be insignificant. For the tests given during confinement, however, the S.D. group was 46 per cent more efficient than the control group, a magnitude of difference that is significant. The control group's efficiency remained unchanged from the first test. The increase in efficiency for the S.D. group did not persist into the postconfinement period.

When it became obvious to our S.D. subjects that they were to be subjected to a series of tests, they spent much of the S.D. time planning how to attack the tasks. On the other hand, the control subjects had other things to do and apparently devoted little or no thought to the taking of learning tests.

One additional analysis was made of these data. Viewing the number of trials required by each subject to meet the criterion of learning, we measured the variability of the two groups, variability being simply a measure of how much the individual scores differed from each other. Before and after confinement the S.D. group was just as variable as the control group.

On the confinement tests, however, the S.D. group was significantly *less* variable than the control group. This finding suggests that the confinement had the effect of making those subjected to it more alike in their learning performance. Thus it seems that the experience of S.D. renders a group of people more homogeneous even in the learning performance.

After all postconfinement tests were completed, we had each subject relearn each list he had received during the entire series, for we reasoned that forgetting should have been reduced during S.D. and that relearning would thus occur more rapidly. Such was not the case; it took just as long for the S.D. group to relearn the list as it did for the control group. I suspect, though, that our hunch was correct but our procedure faulty. We had the subjects relearning so much material at one sitting that the mass of it alone probably provided enough interference to blot out any other effect. The study should be done again, and the material should be presented and partially learned before confinement and then either recalled or relearned to mastery after confinement. A comparable control group should perform the same task. Such an arrangement would at least have a fair chance of demonstrating whether S.D. can improve retention of material. Think of the advantage to learning if we could devise a situation where forgetting is minimized.

CHAPTER X

The Effect of S.D. upon Learning a New Task

In the previous two chapters we have discussed the effects of S.D. upon learning where the task to be learned was similar to many previous learning tasks experienced in the lives of our subjects. Even before we knew the results of those studies, we reasoned that we should investigate the effects of S.D. on a task that was entirely new to the subject. We wanted more than just novel material—the nonsense syllables in the previous task were new to our subjects. We wanted not only novel material but a novel learning procedure, so we selected a mirror drawing task, which was entirely new to all our subjects. The mirror drawing task consists of tracing an outline that one can see only in a mirror. The figure to be traced was of two five-pointed stars, of different sizes, one within the other. The subject's task was to draw a line between the two stars all the way around the pattern without touching the lines of the stars. He could see and thus guide his performance *only* by reference to a mirror.

Mirror images are confusing at best, and real learning must take place in the situation above if the task

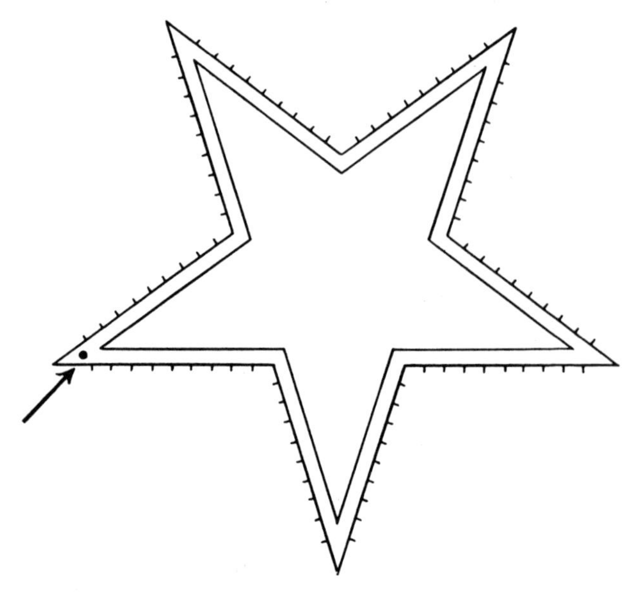

FIG. 5. SUBJECT STARTS AT ARROW AND FINISHES BY GOING ALL THE WAY AROUND THE STAR, BETWEEN THE LINES, AND BACK TO START.

is to be completed. The mirror does not reverse the direction of movements, but it tends to lead the subject to *believe* that it does. If he needs to move to the right he will tend to move to the left, at least early in the task, then he will stop and attempt to correct his error by movement to the right, the direction he should have moved at first, except that now he has probably also moved *up* and to the right, so he must stop and move down, and by now he has forgotten and takes off to the left again. It can be a very confusing task, and some people merely hold the pencil still for long periods of time, unable to move in any direction.

Shaving, and its use of mirrors, does not help one in the mirror drawing problem. Apparently the tactual qualities of the razor and long practice are important to locating the razor on the face and causing it to go where one wishes it to go. Thus shaving is not done exclusively by the mirror image, such as is the case in the drawing task.

There were two scores on this task: the time required to complete the test and the number of errors made. An error was made any time the subject's line touched that of the star pattern. If he crossed a line, two errors were counted. If our subject rushed through the test in order to do it quickly, chances were that he would make more errors; conversely, if he were careful to avoid making errors, it would probably run his time score up. The scoring procedure was explained to each subject.

We investigated the mirror drawing task with twenty-four subjects who were divided equally into S.D. and control subjects. As in previous tests the two main groups were divided into three subgroups, representing twenty-four, forty-eight, and seventy-two hours of confinement. Each S.D. subject received his first test before entering confinement and the second one upon release, meaning that for the twenty-four-hour group, as an example, the two tests were separated by twenty-four hours. Thus a control group was given its two tests separated by twenty-four hours. And so on for the forty-eight- and seventy-two-hour groups.

The table below provides the results of the time measurements. All subjects improved from Test 1 to Test 2; figures are percentages of improvement.

Time Scores, per cent of Improvement of Test 2 over Test 1

Subgroups (in number of hours)	24	48	72
S.D.	51%	17%	58%
Control	55%	49%	50%

First, note that all three control subgroups performed in about the same manner: they improved about 50 per cent, or cut their time in half. We had expected the S.D. subgroups to do even better. We had predicted that the learning from the first test would be better retained during S.D. and thus provide for a greatly improved second performance. This was not the case, for the performance by the forty-eight-hour S.D. subgroups was significantly worse than that of the control subgroups. Note that the other S.D. subgroups (twenty-four-hour and seventy-two-hour) performed very closely to the control group, but for some reason the forty-eight-hour S.D. group did poorly. This poor performance is partially explained by the next set of data.

In the table below, the error scores for each subgroup are provided. Once again all subjects reduced their errors from Test 1 to Test 2 and these data are presented as percentages of improvement.

Error Scores, per cent of Improvement of Test 2 over Test 1

Subgroups (in number of hours)	24	48	72
S.D.	43%	76%	30%
Control	78%	57%	88%

Once again we note that the S.D. group was not better than the control group; in fact it was worse. The control group averaged a 74 per cent improvement, while the S.D. group averaged only 50 per cent improvement. Note, however, that despite the relatively poor showing of the other S.D. subgroups the forty-eight-hour subgroup showed more improvement than the corresponding control subgroup.

It is possible to understand the performances of the forty-eight-hour S.D. subgroup if we consider them together. Apparently this subgroup was able to improve its error scores by sacrificing its time score. This suggests that they strove for accuracy rather than speed. The only question remaining now is: why did only the forty-eight-hour S.D. subgroup perform this way, why not all S.D. subgroups? One possible answer that can be offered here is that S.D. subjects seem to have become especially cautious after forty-eight hours of confinement. Apparently that length of time was considered to be bad by most subjects. It was a point requiring an adjustment on his part, and if he got through that phase he was able to continue confinement. It is reasonable to suggest that caution would naturally be uppermost in his thinking at that time.

Something of an over-all view is provided by combining and averaging the two scores, and a crude measure of total improvement results.

Combined Time and Error Scores (in per cent)

Subgroups (in number of hours)	24	48	72
S.D.	47%	46%	44%
Control	67%	53%	69%

It is not really proper to combine percentage figures in this manner, but it does provide an easy reference to the data. From the table above it can be seen that the control subgroups were consistently better than those of the S.D. All subgroups considered and both measures taken into account, the control subjects improved an average of 63 per cent, while the S.D. subjects improved only 45 per cent. This suggests that, contrary to our expectations, S.D. had a deleterious effect upon the mirror drawing task.

Indicating that S.D. is probably not a suitable place to learn really novel tasks, these findings, limited though they are, may have important applications. Consider the case of an individual who is forced to perform under conditions similar to those of S.D. Such a case might be that of a manned space vehicle.

The pilot probably will not experience a complete deterioration of his skills once in flight, but he may find his performance less than desirable. This condition could probably be avoided if he were trained under conditions highly similar to the real thing. Note that our S.D. subjects had no training *during* S.D. Our hypothetical space pilot will be performing during his confinement; thus he should be trained under conditions of isolation. With this arrangement probably the worst he can expect is a slightly slowed-down rate of learning. It seems reasonable that it would be a mistake to train him for flight skills under one set of conditions and expect him to perform under a different set even though the actual skills required were the same in both cases. I am reminded of a personal experience that illustrates this well. I did poorly on my first solo airplane flight and always felt that it was due to a drastic change in conditions. During dual flights the instructor talked to the student through a "gosport," which was little more than a funnel with two tubes connected to cups fitted over the student's ears. As a communication device it was almost a total failure, but it very effectively masked out a great deal of the engine noise, especially as it was the practice to put the headset on very tightly in an effort to improve hearing. In any case on that eventful day the instructor got out of the airplane, taking the gosport and my headset with him, with the result that I could hear, for the first time, the full intensity of sound coming from that engine, and it proved to be very distracting. Note that in this case no new skills were required. One had only to fly as before. But it was a new skill learned under *different* conditions and was thus easily disrupted. Naturally I may be overimpressed by this simple example, but I propose that when a skill is new and possibly easily disturbed under different circumstances all the possible actual conditions should be incorporated into the learning situation. Additional insurance can be gained by practicing the skill to such a level that it is no longer a *new* skill and thereby decreases its vulnerability to disruption.

Additional investigations are needed before one can recommend the ideal training procedure for, say, an astronaut. It seems reasonable to guess that such studies should look into the effects of isolation. A space capsule on the ground and in flight may provide the same internal environment for the pilot, but on the ground he is not really cut off from his fellow man. True isolation, then, should be incorporated into his training procedures.

PERFORMANCE ON UNSTRUCTURED TASKS

Many investigators have found a large number of S.D. subjects who could not maintain cohesive trains of thought during confinement. It thus seemed important to test the effect of S.D. upon the performance of unstructured cognitive tasks. That is, not the memory of some learned item or items, but thoughts that were not predetermined or practiced or structured in any particular way. It also seemed important to attempt to separate the effects of social isolation from those of sensory deprivation. Three groups of subjects were established: a socially isolated group (S.I. group), where each subject was confined alone for twenty-four hours in a lighted room and with no reduction in sensory stimulation; a sensory deprivation group (S.D. group), which was treated in the usual S.D. manner; and a control group, which was treated similarly to previous control groups. The subjects of the S.I. group could move about, talk to themselves, sing, dance, or do just about anything they wished except interact with other people. In S.D. there is, obviously, in addition to the other restrictions an absence of social exchange. Thus the S.I. group provides a way of evaluating the effects of this restriction alone.

All subjects were given a standardized verbal description of a scene and asked to tell a story about it. (Psychologists will recognize this task as a verbal Thematic Apperception Test). Each subject was encouraged to make his story as detailed as possible, and all stories were recorded. The subjects were then dismissed from the laboratory and told to return at the end of two days. In the meantime they were randomly assigned to one of the three groups.

When the subject returned to the laboratory, one of three things occurred: he was confined in S.D. for twenty-four hours; he was confined in S.I. for twenty-four hours; or he was told that a mistake had been made and that he was to come back at the end of twenty-four hours, according to whether the subject was assigned to the S.D., S.I., or control group.

Just before release from S.D. or S.I. or upon return of the control subject to the laboratory, the subject was asked to invent another story about another verbally presented scene. The total word count of the stories was used as a measure of the ability to maintain thought. The difference between the word count for the first test and the second test was taken as an indication of the effect of the intervening conditions.

The control group showed no change in word count. The S.I. group showed an increase in word count which was statistically significant. The S.D. group, on the other hand, showed a significant decrease in word count.

The data seem to offer two findings. First, they suggest that S.D. does impair the ability to concentrate or maintain thought (granting the manner in which we measured it). And second, the S.I. data suggest that this ability can be improved in the absence of distractions. Apparently some sensory stimulation in excess of that present in S.D. is necessary for proper mental functioning, but when the level of stimulation becomes excessive, as in normal mental functioning, it is not so good as it might otherwise be.

In as much as these effects were produced by only twenty-four hours of treatment, it is logical to guess that an even greater magnitude of effect could be produced by longer confinement times.

PART FOUR

S.D. and the Body

CHAPTER XI

Sensory Deprivation and Hallucinations

"I GUESS I was in there about a day or so before you opened the observation window. I wondered why you waited so long to observe me." This statement was the first example of a hallucination experienced by any of our S.D. subjects. We had expected S.D. to produce hallucinations, as the group working in Dr. Hebb's laboratory at McGill University had reported such occurrences. In fact twenty-five of twenty-nine subjects they used reported some form of them. It will be seen that the specific conditions of isolation become important to this study, so those employed by the McGill group must be reviewed. Their subjects were confined in a cubicle that was continually illuminated by a sixty-watt bulb. It was also air-conditioned, and the sound of the motor could be heard inside the cubicle. The subject wore cardboard gauntlets that extended from below the finger tips to above the elbow. He also wore semitranslucent goggles through which he could distinguish light and dark but was unable to make pattern discernments. The confinement was interrupted for meals and toilet needs.

In one of their studies fourteen subjects reported a variety of visual experiences as having occurred during their confinement. The simple form of visual experience was shifts from light to dark, dots, lines, or simple geometric patterns. All fourteen subjects reported "seeing" such things. A more complex visual experience was seeing something like "wallpaper patterns," which eleven subjects reported. Isolated figures and objects that had no backgrounds were reported by seven of the fourteen. Only three reported integrated complex scenes that were similar to a "cartoon." Some of these hallucinations were tilted at an angle and even, in a few cases, inverted. Some subjects experienced hallucinations other than visual ones. One subject reported hearing people speaking, and another repeatedly heard a music box. There were also tactual hallucinations. One subject "saw" a tiny ship firing pellets and felt them strike his arm. Another "saw" a doorknob and reached out for it, only to receive a mild electric shock in his fingers. Thus he also hallucinated the feeling of the doorknob.

Our first S.D. study, which utilized only four subjects, did not reveal any visual hallucinations. This came as something of a surprise, for all fourteen of the McGill subjects had at least the "simple form" of visual experience. Thus we were led to consider carefully the differences in the conditions of confinement for the two studies. We decided that our study was "at fault," for patterned vision by means of a red light had been allowed during mealtimes. We changed our conditions so that no light occurred in the cubicle. The subjects had everything in the cubicle they needed except toilet facilities, and when that need arose they were blindfolded and let out of the cubicle to a toilet. Under these conditions we used nine subjects. Six of these experienced a total of fifteen hallucinations.

WHAT IS A HALLUCINATION?

The definition of a hallucination is a pretty tricky affair. Webster describes it as an apparent perception without an external cause, an adequate definition except that it does not distinguish hallucinations from vivid daydreaming. In the case of our subject mentioned at the beginning of the chapter, he reported that he "saw" a window. Couldn't he have just as easily imagined or daydreamed or "invented" the window? It's a touchy problem in this case to separate imagination from hallucination, as one must necessarily depend upon the verbal report of the subject. It has occurred to me that perhaps the technique of recording eye movements might help identify true hallucinations. Presumably hallucinations are "out there" in space and the eyes should scan the scene presented to them. The most likely difficulty with this procedure is that the subject's eyes will be open and naturally move about. But perhaps the two types of eye movements could be distinguished; if so, this technique might help separate hallucinations from vivid day-dreams.

We wanted to be as careful as possible in deciding what to call a hallucination, and we adopted the criteria of earlier workers in this field of study. Guiraud, a French psychiatrist working in the early nineteenth century, specialized in the hallucinations of the mentally ill. As he used the nature of the hallucination to identify the source of the illness, it was essential that he rigidly demand a correct identification of the phenomenon. Guiraud kindly gave credit to earlier investigators, but he laid down the rules by which hallucinations have since been identified. His rules were: (1) the experience must have an "out-thereness," just like any visual experience of the real world, (2) the one experiencing the hallucination must be able to scan, to attend selectively to, the various parts of the experience, (3) it must not be producible at the will of the subject, (4) the subject must not be able to terminate it, and (5) it must, for all purposes, "fool" the observer with its realism. These were the criteria adopted by us.

In the postconfinement interview we attempted to determine whether our subject had hallucinated in S.D. We had to be very careful, for it was essential not to suggest that we *expected* him to hallucinate. If subjects had been given that idea, chances are that most of them would have done their best to come up with something that could have been called a hallucination.

We had expected to have problems with any subject experiencing them. For one thing, these phenomena are associated with disease, drugs, alcohol, high temperature, mental disorder, etc. Thus we thought that our subjects might be afraid to report any such "damaging" testimony to us. As it turned out, our fears were ungrounded. To a man, if our subjects hallucinated they volunteered the information before we questioned them, and they spoke freely. They were not only unembarrassed about their hallucinations, they readily admitted enjoying them as welcome relief. When their perceptions disappeared or faded away, most subjects tried unsuccessfully to bring them back.

CLASSIFICATION OF HALLUCINATIONS

We attempted to classify hallucinations in order to facilitate comparisons among the various studies. We decided that there were three visual types: "*Type 1 hallucination,*" the simplest imaginable visual experience, consisted of flashes of light, flickering lights, shimmering, and the like, experiences that were always confined to the peripheral field of view and that, try as a subject might, could not be fixated. *Type 2 hallucination* was a little more complex; it was in the central field of view, it could be fixated, and it consisted primarily of geometrical patterns or was easily reducible to geometry. *Type 3 hallucination* was the fully integrated complex scene that might even include motion and clearly could not be reduced to geometric figures.

According to our system of classification, all fourteen McGill subjects experienced Types 1 and 2, and ten of the fourteen had Type 3.

In our study, using nine subjects, six of the nine had a total of fifteen hallucinations. Nine of the fifteen were of Type 1, six were of Type 2, and there were *no* Type 3 hallucinations.

The Type 2 hallucinations were very plain and unexciting affairs. One subject, already mentioned, saw a window. The window was easily reducible to a rectangle containing a series of squares. It is interesting in this particular case that our subject saw what he expected—that we would look in on him—and he was surprised only that we had not done it earlier in his confinement.

Another subject saw a ventilator in the ceiling. Once again here is the element of expectation, for the ventilator, as he drew it, was composed of a large, narrow rectangle filled with many smaller rectangles.

One subject reported seeing a piece of soundproofing hanging in front of him. When asked to draw it he drew a net composed of small diamond shapes. He thought that a sheet of the soundproofing had come loose from the ceiling and was hanging down in front of him.

Another subject reported seeing a dime on the floor. At first he thought that an accidental light leak had developed in the room and that the light was being reflected by the dime. As he reached for it it disappeared, much to his disappointment. When the coin reappeared to him later, he resisted the temptation to pick it up, hoping to make it last longer. To his sorrow it once again faded quickly.

At this point we somewhat naturally got the idea that by having increased the severity of S.D. we had begun to generate hallucinations. We then set out to make the conditions even more severe and we did so by providing the cubicle with relief bottles and the antechamber with a chemical toilet. With this arrangement, which we continue to use at present, we ran nine more subjects. To our very great surprise only one subject had a *single example* of what might be classified as a hallucination. There's even some doubt that it was one. He saw the edge of a meat sandwich glow; as it had been in the food chest for three days, it might have become tainted and produced some sort of a glow. Even if we allow that experience to be called a hallucination, the incidence of them was at a much lower frequency than we had expected.

The puzzling question was: Why should those in the previous study experience hallucinations and not those in the last study? The major difference between them was that the first group came out of S.D. to use the toilet. Breaking up S.D. in that fashion should have minimized the confinement and hence been less likely to produce hallucination, or so we thought. We called the original nine subjects back to the laboratory and after extensive questioning and blind groping we stumbled onto what was probably an important fact. All of these subjects found the blindfold, used when they went to the toilet, to be inadequate. In each case there were small light leaks around the edges of the blindfold so that their eyes were stimulated by light. In every case they indicated that they could not see anything by the light—they just saw light. Now it will be recalled that Dr. Hebb's subjects saw light and no form also. Beginning subsequent studies, we reasoned that the crucial features of the work at McGill University were the light and the goggles, which did not allow pattern discrimination. The data seem to hang together, so we did the obvious thing next, the designing of a situation that would permit light in as homogeneous a manner as possible. Instead of goggles we fashioned Ping-pong balls to fit over the eyes. Thus the bridge of the nose or the edge of the cheek would not be in the visual field. We borrowed this technique from Dr. Julian Hochberg and his associates, who at an earlier time had investigated color vision. He projected the visual stimulus through the small hemispheres in order to present a uniform visual field. Incidentally, some of his subjects reported seeing shapes and forms (which of course were not there) in addition to colors. They even insisted that these things were part of the experiment.

We attached the Ping-pong-ball hemispheres over the eyes with moleskin, a cloth-like mastic similar to a sheet of adhesive tape. The illumination, which was attached directly to the subject's head so that it would be constant in intensity even as he moved his head, was provided by a large section of Panelescent, made by Sylvania Electric Products as a night light, and this was attached to a headband and bent around as a mask in front of the Ping-pong balls. In this way we hoped to maximize visual stimulation but at the same time prevent patterned or form vision. The light provided a faint blue-green color.

We confined ten subjects for forty-eight hours. At the very maximum only two subjects reported hallucinations, which in all cases were Type 3. One subject saw a "cogwheel turning slowly" and a "city skyline," while the other saw "a river with floating white balls," "a floral wallpaper design," and "a stone archway." These hallucinations were very brief, lasting a very few seconds.

Considering the results of the McGill study and our own study that had the light leaks, the above findings came as a surprise, and we decided to add the one other feature present in the McGill study—that of a constant noise. We arranged a white-noise generator (which produces a mixture of all audible frequencies) to play into earplugs that were fitted comfortably and snugly into the ears. By using the plugs we provided a more homogeneous sound field, for the subject could not change it by moving his head or placing a pillow over his head and the like, which would have been the case with an outside fixed sound source. Each subject received the sound at forty db above his threshold of hearing, producing a level of sound about as loud as that of the average office.

This study was conducted the same as before, and all conditions of light, duration, etc., were the same except for the addition of the sound. None of the eleven subjects under these conditions had hallucinations. Thus we are back where we had started, only now more confused than ever. At one point we thought that, to produce hallucinations in S.D., we had only to present an amorphous visual stimulation, but now we know that such is not an adequate condition. It is possible that we made our conditions of light and sound *too* homogeneous so that there was not enough differentiation. It is possible that we didn't confine them for enough time, although I doubt this and will explain presently. It is clear to me that we have only begun to penetrate the field of visual hallucinations and that at present we are suffering one of the many setbacks that plague research.

Before turning to the next study, we should make one comment about the light used in the last two studies. It will be recalled that the constant light presented a faint blue-green color. All subjects reported that the light soon lost its blue-green cast and became a dark gray, but oddly enough the color could be briefly restored by an eye blink. Once restored it faded again very quickly. This unusual little phenomenon not only is of interest in itself, but serves to illustrate that our best-laid plans for complete homogeneity of light were less than perfect.

Another unusual, interesting, and unexplained finding was the absence of an afterimage, which is the persistence of any visual stimulation after it has been removed; this is a process that goes on within the visual apparatus. Everyone has experienced visual afterimages when he first looks at a light and then turns it off. Although the room becomes dark, we tend to continue seeing the extinguished light.

Under the conditions of our previous two studies we should have produced some pronounced afterimages when the Panelescent was turned off at the end of the confinement. We even instructed the subjects to look long and hard for afterimages, but this proved to be of no avail.

For our next study we decided to maximize the "light leak" condition, which had previously given the greatest frequency of hallucinations. This time we wanted to be sure that all subjects were in fact stimulated by light. We also wanted to be sure that the light did not allow patterned vision, and we wanted intermittent light. These, we felt, were the critical features.

The visual stimulus was shown on a screen at the foot of the subject's bed. It was composed of smears of pastel chalk that became luminescent when black light was directed upon it. This technique had the advantage that nothing else in the cubicle was illuminated. The visual display when activated had the amorphous and somewhat tridimensional appearance of a dark, starry night. The panel was activated by the experimenter for at least two one-second periods every eight hours of confinement. Ten subjects were confined for forty-eight hours each. One subject reported experiencing hallucinations. Not only did he experience every variety of hallucinations, but he had an unbelievably large number of them. He reported a total of ninety-six visual experiences, of which eighteen were Type 3 hallucinations, eleven were Type 2, and twelve were Type 1. The other forty-five reports were that "the level of illumination in the room has changed," when he was actually in every case in total darkness. The great frequency of this subject's reporting may be more an indication of his need to maintain contact with the experimenter than a measure of his hallucinatory activity.

Each of our studies seems not only to have failed to create maximum conditions for the generation of visual hallucinations, but to have uncovered some additional interesting side lights. The previous study is no exception. All of the ten subjects reported that they "saw" the panel, in front of them, being illuminated from a position behind their heads. They did not "assume" that the source of illumination was behind them: each had the distinct impress of "seeing" it that way. Actually the panel was illuminated from its bottom edge and in no way involved any other part of the S.D. cubicle. We are at a loss to explain this effect, especially as none of the subjects knew of the visual display in advance.

Investigators in addition to those at McGill University have reported such greater frequency of hallucinatory activity in S.D. than we did. We have subjected a total of fifty-five subjects to various kinds of S.D. and found only ten who experienced hallucinations.

In the McGill studies twenty-five out of twenty-nine subjects hallucinated. The studies at Wright-Patterson Air Force Base by Dr. Ruff *et al.* are as lacking in positive findings as ours. They found hallucinations in only two out of sixty subjects. Dr. Wexler, working with the tank-type respirator for confinement, found three hallucinators out of seventeen subjects. Drs. Solomon and Mendelson, using the same kind of respirator-tank confinement, found seven of twenty-eight subjects experiencing hallucinations. In some cases the hallucinations appeared after only 1.25 hours of confinement, while for others it was after sixteen hours. Dr. Cohen *et al.*, the investigators at Duke University, found seven out of ten subjects reporting hallucinations even though the duration of S.D. was only two hours.

Three studies using a very different approach to S.D. also report a high incidence of hallucinatory activity. These experiments have suspended their subjects in a tank of water. The original work was done at the National Institutes of Health by Dr. John Lilly and has since been followed up by Dr. Jay Shirley at Oklahoma University and Dr. Camberarc at the University of Utah. Dr. Lilly and others who used the immersion technique reasoned that the sense of touch is a very important one and can produce a great deal of stimulation. The ordinary S.D. conditions do not in any way eliminate the sense of touch, but if all skin areas are subjected to equal pressure there is no resulting sensation of it. We ordinarily feel pressure only at the point of pressure change. For example, the finger immersed in water affords the sensation of pressure only at the junction of the air and water. The submerged part of the finger, having uniform pressure, does not afford a sensation of it. During the tank experiments the water was kept at a constant temperature so as to eliminate sensations of warmth and coldness, the breathing mask fitted to each subject produced audible breathing sounds, and any movements by him were readily appreciative. It was also possible to hear the sound of the water being pumped into the tank to render the temperature constant.

Drs. Zubeck, Pushkar, Sansom, Gowing, and Prysiazniuk, working at the University of Manitoba, used conditions similar to some used by us. They confined sixteen subjects in a dark, soundproof chamber for periods of one week each. They found eleven of the sixteen experiencing some sort of hallucinatory activity. It is notable that these investigators used the criteria for hallucinations which we had insisted upon in a publication with which they were familiar. They also indicate, and this may be very significant, that their subjects did not usually hallucinate before the *third day* of sensory deprivation. Most of their subjects had Type 1 hallucinations, a few Type 2, and only two occasions of Type 3. Both of the Type 3 hallucinations occurred during the *sixth* day of S.D. These investigators also found a number of very realistic auditory hallucinations, such as "howling dogs," "alarm clock," "typewriter," "whistle," "dripping water," etc. Twelve of their subjects were male, ten of whom had hallucinations, while only one of the four female subjects had hallucinations. More information is needed before one can state a clear difference between males and females in their susceptibility to hallucinating in S.D. It is essential for the subjects to understand that the pressure of hallucinations does not mean loss of mentality or anything else of a negative nature.

It seems to me that Dr. Zubeck and his workers may have discovered the essential feature that our work had missed, namely, that the length of S.D. needs to be greater than we used in order to maximize the production of visual hallucinations. We looked again at our findings that produced the most hallucinations—the earlier study of light leaks in the blindfolds. Of the fifteen hallucinations produced, three occurred in the first day of confinement, five in the second day, and seven in the third day. The increased frequency with longer confinement is somewhat in line with Dr. Zubeck's idea.

Dr. Freeman and co-workers at Harvard Medical School offer another explanation for our lack of positive finds here. They claim that the studies finding a high frequency of hallucinatory activity have also involved a great deal of restraint of the subject. They claim our subjects had relative mobility. Actually, while they were not physically restrained to the bed, they were instructed to stay on it except for food and toilet needs and to lie as still as comfortably possible. Nevertheless I suspect that Dr. Freeman may have a good point—restraint causes stress, which may well be related to ease in producing hallucinations. Although the Harvard investigators admit that comparisons of the various studies are "highly tentative," it seems reasonable that their idea of restraint should be tested in a more direct fashion.

AUDITORY HALLUCINATIONS

As a hallucination must by definition have an absence of external physical stimulation, it is very difficult to determine auditory hallucinations. We can be sure about excluding visual stimulation, but to exclude sound is much more difficult. Furthermore, when a good job has been done eliminating external sounds, there remains the problem of internal body noises, which cannot be turned off or shut out. There are heart noises, breathing noises, sounds made by the middle-ear muscles, stomach rumblings, and the like. Any of these sounds might be misinterpreted by the S.D. subject and reported as auditory hallucinations, which for this reason have been difficult to handle. For example, many if not most of our subjects reported that during S.D. they heard "soft rain." (Remember that Dr. Zubeck's subjects heard "dripping water.") A few have reported hearing "trucks rumble" by on the highway, and some have heard the "low drone" of airplanes overhead. While these sounds do actually occur, none of them could possibly have penetrated into the S.D. cubicle. Are these expected sounds that result from the mistaken identification of actual body sounds, or are they auditory hallucinations?

We tried to shed some light on this problem by deliberately suggesting that the subjects in S.D. would hear something. Just before he entered the cubicle we told him that we would occasionally pipe snatches of music into the chamber to help relieve the monotony. We said that it was not part of the study but that he might try to identify the music he heard. In the experimenter's area, where the subject was made ready for S.D., we placed a record player and records, with wires leading into the cubicle to substantiate our hoax.

No one was fooled. Of the nine subjects treated in this manner all came out of S.D. complaining that we forgot to play the music. Some of them did report soft rain and truck rumblings, however. In the case of the ten subjects (mentioned earlier) who had white noise in their ears during confinement there were no reports of auditory hallucinations. About the only effect of the thermal noise was for some few who found that the noise delayed sleep slightly and for a most unusual reason. They noted that as they were dropping off to sleep the sound of the noise cutoff and the loud silence awakened them in a very abrupt manner and usually happened several times before they finally went to sleep. In a more casual way I have noted the same effect while driving late at night. The sound of the car motor will "cut off" as I doze off to sleep, and this loud silence always awakens me. It makes one feel that the sensory departments stop acting just in advance of losing consciousness.

FUTURE STUDIES OF HALLUCINATION

Attempts to generate hallucinations during S.D. might well lead to the problem of stress and people's reactions to it. For some people S.D. is an event of great stress—so much so that they demand an early release. It is also known that stress of a different form can produce hallucinations. The person stranded on a life raft may eventually come to hallucinate, people lost in a desert or in the arctic—all have been known to produce very elaborate hallucinations. Of course it must be kept in mind that those are life-and-death situations, whereas S.D. is not.

I must admit that there have been no more hallucinations among those who requested early release from S.D. than those who did not. Nevertheless I tend to feel that the element of increased stress should be investigated. This could be done by effecting a more clear-cut isolation, leading the subject to believe that he is alone in the area and that no experimenters are monitoring him except at a great distance. We could also build in minor accidents, such as not including enough water, increasing the heat and humidity or doing other things to make the subject more stressed and at the same time have the other conditions necessary for producing hallucinations. It would be easier, of course, if we knew precisely what these other conditions are, though we state some conditions that do not work and can make some guesses about some that might work.

The first results of investigating the effect of hallucinations generated in S.D. are now in. Mr. William Rust, working in our laboratories, stressed one group of confined subjects while leaving another group unstressed. The production of stress was accomplished by the instructions read to the subject. For example they were told that the S.D. situation resembled the Chinese brainwashing situation and that in general it was a stressful affair. The subjects to whom such a description was present were found to be more anxious about S.D. than the control subjects when tested by questionaire. That is to say, the attempt to introduce stress was successful.

It was expected that the stressed group would hallucinate while the control group would not. Such, however, was not the case; neither group hallucinated. It might be argued that the stress produced in the present case was too mild. Or perhaps stress must be in conjunction with some of the other features we have previously tried, such as light leaks, etc. In any event, it is clear that we have not reached closure on this matter, and so the work will continue.

CHAPTER XII

Some Physical Effects of Sensory Deprivation

EARLIER mention was made of the book *Sensory Deprivation*, edited by Philip Solomon and others. That book grew out of a symposium and is comprised of contributions from many investigators, including the author, in the area of S.D. The work we will consider here is presented in some detail in Chapter IV of that book.

Many of our subjects upon release from S.D. have remarked that they felt "unsteady" on their feet, "unsure of movements," "not well co-ordinated," etc. These comments caused us to try to measure the effects of S.D. upon motor performance.

RAIL-WALKING ABILITY

We attempted to measure the ability of our subjects to walk accurately. The rail-walking test we used is much like what its name implies. A pattern of wooden rails was arranged in an open U shape eighteen feet in total length. The subject was required to stand erect, hands at sides, and walk the rail in his stockinged feet.

If he stepped off the rail, he had to start over. The time he took to negotiate the total distance was the measurement of his performance.

For the first test eighteen subjects were graded on their ability to walk the rail and, according to their performance, they were divided into two groups of nine each. One group became the control, or comparison group, and the other the S.D. group, each selected so that the two were fairly equal in the ability to walk the rail.

The S.D. group was confined in the cubicle for periods up to seventy-two hours and took a second test upon release, the control group receiving its second test after comparable periods of time. Though this was a very simple task, there was some slight improvement on the part of the control group at its second testing. On the average it was 8 per cent better than at the first test. The S.D. group, on the other hand, not only did not improve, but on the average was 42 per cent worse.

These findings suggest that S.D. experience does have an undesirable effect upon even a very simple motor task. The problem that remains unanswered is the duration of such effects. With some certainty it can be said that these disruptive effects are not permanent, but additional study is needed to determine the time required for recovery.

MOTOR CO-ORDINATION

Our next test was one requiring a higher degree of

skill than the rail-walking test. It was our hope to measure the effects of S.D. upon more skilled motor performances. The task was the rotary-pursuit test, which measures one's ability to maintain contact with a small disc on a moving circle. Imagine a penny placed upon a moving phonograph record; and the problem is to keep a wire in contact with the coin. It sounds simple, but keeping contact with the coin for twenty seconds out of a one-minute trial period is considered very good.

Subjects were tested and divided into two groups of nearly equal ability. All of the control subjects showed improvement in their performances on the second test. Most of the S.D. subjects showed improvement on their postconfinement, or second, test. The subjects who did not improve were those confined for forty-eight hours. Their postconfinement test was about the same (actually slightly less) than their preconfinement test, whereas they should have shown a significant improvement.

This suggests once again that forty-eight hours of S.D. is a significant length of confinement that in many cases is more disruptive than longer periods.

HAND TREMOR

The final measure we attempted is a very obvious one. People who are stressed or excited, anxious or disturbed, or are in certain other states very often display an increase in hand trembling. Thus, confident that we could predict the results, we planned to measure the hand tremor of our S.D. subjects—nine who were to be confined for ninety-six hours—before and after confinement.

Hand tremor was measured by requiring the subject to hold a small metal stylus of 1/8″ diameter within a hole of 3/8″ diameter in a metal plate, the plate and stylus electrically wired so that each contact between them activated a timer. The less time accumulated on the timer, the better the performance and hence the steadier the hand.

The expected results did not obtain. The S.D. subjects were no worse or no less steady after their confinement than before. In fact they were not only the same as they had been, they were just like the comparison group. There were nine S.D. subjects, but only six completed the full four days; the three others pushed the panic button and requested early release. When we looked at the hand-tremor data according to whether the subject was successful, significant changes became apparent. The group who completed the full four days showed a statistically significant *increase* in hand tremor for the postconfinement test, while the unsuccessful group showed a statistically significant *decrease*. Obviously, when considered as a single group, these two opposite trends had canceled each other. It would appear that if there is sufficient S.D. it will reflect in a negative fashion in such primitive indicators as hand tremor.

The surprising thing is that the data were not reversed. One would expect the unsuccessful group to have been less steady and shown greater tremor. Perhaps the relief of release from S.D., which each had found so intolerable, was enough to have a calming effect.

REACTION TIME

The final test we conducted in measuring physiological capacities was that of reaction time, which, simply stated, is the speed of performance of an act. In our test the subject was instructed to flip a switch as quickly as possible after a signal light came on. Turning on the light started a clock, and the subject's response stopped it. His reaction time was measured to 1/1000 of a second. The average reaction time to such a light signal would be from 0.150 to 0.225 seconds.

Our fifteen subjects were to be confined for ninety-six hours each. Their reaction time before confinement was, on the average, 0.174 seconds and upon release averaged 0.175 seconds. Thus it would appear that S.D. had no effect upon reaction time. However, the same thing happened here as with hand tremor. Of the fifteen subjects only seven completed the full four days: the other eight requested early release. The reaction time for the successful group was essentially the same, that is, unchanged by S.D. The unsuccessful group was a different matter, for it showed a statistically significant decrease in the speed of its reaction time. Since reaction time is usually a fairly stable measure, the suggestion here is that something important has happened to the subject who was unsuccessful in S.D. Once again it is necessary to say that the duration of this negative effect is unknown, but that in all probability it is not a permanent one.

CHAPTER XIII

Perception of Pain

A RESEARCH project in its initial phase often starts out by asking "I-wonder-what-will-happen" questions. Such a procedure is in contrast to that used in areas of established knowledge, where the investigator makes a specific hypothesis and proceeds to test it. Because S.D. is a relatively new field of investigation, most of its projects have been of the "I-wonder-what-will-happen" type. A good case in point is the following study on the perception of pain.

We often found that our considerations of S.D. were influenced by reports on various brainwashing procedures, reports indicating that physical violence was often used, despite popular belief to the contrary. Thus we naturally came to question whether the conditions of S.D. would alter the perception of physical pain, whether the same pain hurts more or less in S.D. than normally.

Before describing our techniques and the results let us consider pain briefly. Apparently, pain should be useful to us by providing survival value. The presence of pain serves to warn us about undesirable conditions of health and elements we should avoid. This warning system is arranged so that it can come from practically all areas of the body, though it may do it in various ways. Some body areas are relatively insensitive to pain, while others are capable of extreme pain. For example a scratch on the finger is only mildly painful when compared with a scratch on the eye. A slight amount of heat applied to the skin may be painful, but not nearly so painful as the heat applied inside a tooth by the dental drill. The area around the eardrum is also capable of producing intense pain, while the center of the cheek is almost insensitive to pain. At first glance it would seem that we are carefully provided with abundant pain in the areas of the body so essential to our everyday life. This may be true, but I feel that the job was overdone, for the pain is often so abundant as to frighten people away from proper health measures. Care of the teeth provides an all too frequent example of just such a case. Repair of teeth is, in many cases, so painful as to cause people to avoid it, thus the elaborate warning system comes to help destroy what it was designed to protect. At first encounter, which is usually in impressionable early childhood, one learns that the dentist's chair can be an unpleasant place. Thus the topic of pain perception must include not only pure pain but what we have learned through experience about it.

No matter how we might wish to change nature, the simple fact of pain exists. It is something we have all experienced and will continue to experience. That pain is a prevalent feature of man's life is easily testified by the yearly sales volume of aspirin and other analgesics.

In everyday life it is very easy to produce pain. One has only to cut, burn, or freeze, scratch, tear, or bruise. But in the laboratory we cannot use such techniques. These common agents of pain are of no use there for the simple reason that they cannot be measured. How, for example, would one determine the amount of a cut that produces a threshold of pain? Or how could one apply the same amount of pain repeatedly? Clearly such stimuli do not easily lend themselves to precise measurement. Fortunately for this purpose there is one stimulus that not only can produce pain but can be *measured* and *manipulated* in a very precise manner. That stimulus is electricity, which can do more than merely produce pain. If it is applied in proper amounts to the proper places, it can produce a variety of sensations. When applied through the eyes one "sees" lights, flashes, and flickers. When applied across the ears one "hears" it, and obviously one can feel it when it stimulates the skin. Also when it is applied to the body in moderate amounts, it does not impart any damage to the tissue, a characteristic that is a great advantage for the kind of work we wanted to do. It meant that we would be able to restimulate the same spot of skin repeatedly, and it was only by being able to do this that we could obtain a sound basis for comparison, for the sensitivity of the skin varies greatly from one place to another. Our plan was simply to measure the pain threshold for our S.D. subjects before and after confinement.

The electrical stimulus was applied to the ear lobe. The ear lobe is an ideal area of the body on which to study pain. It yields a very clear impression of pain as a threshold sensation when the proper kind of electrical stimulus is utilized. One simple precaution is necessary, however: The electrical stimulus must be of a relatively low frequency. It need not be so low in frequency as ordinary household electricity, which is sixty cycles per second (cps) but it should be under two thousand cps. It is a peculiar characteristic of the ear lobe that high-frequency electrical stimuli produce not pain but a mildly pleasant and completely painless sensation of vibration, whereas low-frequency stimuli applied to the same area produce pain. The ear lobe offers another advantage for electrical stimulation. It does not perspire; there is thus little change in the electrical conductivity during the investigation.

The stimulus was applied to the ear lobe by two small round electrodes seven millimeters in diameter. They were clamped in place somewhat in the fashion of a woman's earring. The weight of the connecting wires and the electrode holder was supported by a pulley arrangement on a headband worn by the subject, otherwise the weight would have distracted our subjects from detecting the true threshold.

Our task was to find the absolute threshold of electrical pain on the ear lobe of each subject. *Absolute threshold* is arrived at by a standardized procedure: A threshold is the least amount of stimulus that is just detected. It is a statistical concept because it varies, is never really the same from moment to moment, and because the human organism's properties do not stay put. Thus it has become a practice to define *absolute threshold* as that value of the stimulus which is detected just 50 per cent of the time.

We presented our subjects with a large number of stimuli that varied in intensity from well below to just above threshold. These were arranged in random order, and to each brief presentation the subject merely indicated whether he felt it. In this manner we took hundreds of readings on our subjects in a period of six or seven days. From these reports we calculated the minimum stimulus each subject could detect 50 per cent of the time. The results of the study on pain are presented in the table below:

	Average Pain Threshold	
	S.D. Group	Control Group
Test 1	290 microamperes*	240 microamperes
Test 2	182	221
Difference	−108	−19

*A microampere is one millionth of an ampere.

From the data in the table the following conclusions were drawn: First, the two groups started out with similar thresholds; they were not statistically different.

When they were retested four days later, however, they were significantly different. Both groups averaged a decrease in pain threshold (which means an increase in pain sensitivity), but the S.D. group had a greater decrease than the control group; indeed the decrease of the control group was not statistically significant. The S.D. group had a drop of 42 per cent of the original threshold value, while the control group's drop was only 5 per cent.

Of the nine S.D. subjects only one failed to show an increase in sensitivity to pain (or decrease in threshold) after S.D. On the other hand, four of the subjects of the control group showed slight decreases in sensitivity, while five showed slight increases in their second test. Even if we consider only those control subjects who produced an increase in sensitivity, we still have a group that is significantly *less* sensitive to pain than the confined group after S.D. The conclusion is that after S.D. the confined subjects were considerably more sensitive to pain.

How can we explain the effects of S.D. upon pain thresholds? Why should S.D. produce a greater sensitivity to pain? With the control group we might expect people's sensitivity to pain to vary somewhat, but the change was not nearly so great as that found for the S.D. group. Any explanation of these results then will have to include considerations beyond the skin. Though the ear-lobe skin was the locus of the pain stimulus, it is not possible that S.D. produces any changes in it, for it is difficult to alter the skin, short of drastic steps. For example, it is next to impossible, in normal circumstances, to change the temperature of the skin. Thus while the S.D. chamber temperature usually increased from 70° to 76° during occupancy, such a change did not increase the skin's temperature. The relative humidity of the cubicle usually increased from 68 per cent to 71 per cent, but there was no apparent reason why this should change the skin's pain threshold. The explanation of our finding appears to be elsewhere. I would like to venture a possible solution that involves not the skin but the brain. This would be an experiment that borrows heavily from the work of others. It would involve a very special part of the brain called the *reticular formation,* which is not a glamorous executive level of the brain, but is a bulbous development of the spinal cord near the base of the brain. Despite its low station it has connections that lead back and forth to the cortex, which is the outermost layer of the brain, to other body parts. The reticular formation can activate the cortex, which in turn can activate the reticular formation. Nerve impulses travel into the reticular formation from the various sensory organs and are then relayed to the cortex. The sensory organs also send neural impulses directly to the cortex, but that those traveling directly, it has been proposed, will not be received unless the reticular system arouses the cortex to activity. It is as though the reticular system were a gatekeeper for the cortex, as though it gets the brain ready to receive neural messages. If the ascending neural fibers leading from the reticular formation up to the cortex are cut, the organism passes into a coma-like state from which there is no arousal. On the other hand the descending neural fibers that lead from the cortex down to the reticular formation can exert an influence upon other neural messages coming into the reticular formation. They may block out some other impulse. Thus the reticular formation may be viewed as something of a governor controlling the activity of the brain. When we are intent upon one activity, it may be the reticular formation that prevents distractions from coming to our attention. Evidence of this kind of thinking comes from the work of Drs. Hernández-Peón, Scherrer, and Jouvet, a team of Spanish physiologists. They placed recording electrodes in the auditory system of the brain of a cat. When sound stimulated the cat, the electrodes detected the resulting neural activity, which could be viewed on a cathode ray oscillograph. These investigators found that the recorded neural activity to sounds could be blocked by merely allowing the cat to see a rat, data suggesting that at the sight of the rat the cat's interest was aroused and its neural activity directed accordingly. Part of that act was to block out the neural impulses aroused by the sound stimuli. There is one complication with these findings, which is that a cat, by moving its head, may have either changed the sound field or may have moved to an area where there was actually less sound. A continuously present sound, even a series of clicks, will produce *standing waves* in a closed room. These standing waves when in phase will summate to produce a louder sound and when out of phase will produce a greatly decreased sound. By experimentation it has been found that in some cases moving as little as the thickness of a cat's head can produce as much as a twenty-five-db change in the sound level. These findings tend to cast some doubt on the work of Dr. Hernández-Peón and his colleagues. Dr. Hernández-Peón suggests that the blocking occurred at the level of the reticular formation. In simple form the process is here suggested: The cat allows the auditory messages to come into the brain when nothing better is offered. But the instant the rat appears the cat is actively interested in the rat and nothing else. Therefore the cortex, through the descending tracks to the reticular formation, blocks the incoming neural signals initiated by the sound stimulus down at the level of the reticular formation, so that these messages do not reach the higher levels of the brain. When the rat is removed the neural messages from the sounds once again get through the brain.

If we can accept the work cited above, we then see a mechanism in the brain which may inhibit certain neural messages coming into it. The activity resulting from one sensory department may serve to block and/or inhibit the efforts produced by another sense department.

In as much as the brain is always active from stimulation of the various sense departments, we may suggest that there is a continual partial blocking to the neural effects resulting from sensory stimulation. The system may be normally partially "overloaded," possibly reducing its efficiency in dealing with any specific neural event. The possibility of this normal mild cortical blocking may be reduced in S.D. for the simple reason that the sensory stimulation is greatly reduced. If the blocking action is reduced, the result may be an increased ability to perceive incoming events. Thus after a period of S.D. the neural events that resulted from the pain stimuli encountered less blocking and were thereby able to produce sensations at a lower level of intensity.

Admittedly there is a great deal of speculation involved in the explanation of the effect of S.D. upon the perception of pain. At present information about the reticular formation is new and incomplete, but until other studies are brought forward our explanation remains a possibility. There are many everyday examples where pain goes undetected because of other events. For example, the fisherman may fail to note a badly cut foot in the excitement of landing a "really big one." A soldier, in the heat of battle, has often completely overlooked a serious wound. The injury in each case is not lessened by the distraction and the pain receptors must have acted in their usual manner, but the pain was not felt. Apparently the pain was blocked at the reticular formation by the other actions of the cortex, which in these examples demanded the subjects' full attention. One cannot help wonder if this is the mechanism by which hypnosis can prevent pain.

Our study for the effects of S.D. upon pain thresholds brings up other questions. For example, how much S.D. is required to effect a change in pain thresholds? We used four days of S.D. and obtained a 42-per-cent change; would one day yield a 10-per-cent change? Would longer periods of S.D. or more severe forms of S.D. lead to even greater changes? Is it also possible that other perceptions would be equally affected?

From our research we can offer some tentative guesses about tolerance to pain in brainwashing—mentioned earlier in the chapter. It is reasonable to suggest that increased pain sensitivity would reduce tolerance to pain, for it would be the same as increasing the intensity of pain. A mild pain does not debilitate, as one can endure it and even carry on normal activity, but more severe pain will at first distract and finally become a totally engrossing affair. Under conditions of S.D. a person subjected to brainwashing might become more vulnerable to pain.

The effects of S.D. on pain could likely be effectively counteracted. As we have already seen, pain often goes unnoticed because of distractions, and it is suggested here that any pain we suffer can be reduced by deliberately arranging distraction. It may be for just this reason that illness so often overtakes us at night during sleep. The neural signals of illness must occur in daytime as often as at night, but they are more likely to go unnoticed during our normal daytime activity. At night-time there is so little distraction that such signals can more easily get through the reticular system and register in consciousness.

To produce distractions for pain deliberately would not be so easy in a confinement situation as in normal life, but it can nevertheless be done. Even if the conditions of the confinement were so severe as to offer no other possible distraction, it would still be possible to divert the subject's attention. If all else is prevented, pain is capable of distracting itself. Pain is an experience about which we know very little. When we experience it we merely judge it to be undesirable, but we don't know what it is like beyond that "it hurts." We can change this by deliberately attempting to observe pain. If one attempts to become familiar with pain so as to render good subjective descriptions of it, the unpleasantness of it will be reduced. An objective attitude toward specific pain tends to reduce the emotional trauma, the shock, and thus reduce the general unpleasantness of it. If one actively *desires* to observe a phenomenon, he is less likely to wish for its end. The reader may try this technique on his next trip to the dentist or during his next headache. With a little practice it may produce surprising results.

It is conceivable that this technique of reducing pain by observing it would be easier to perform in S.D. than in normal life, for S.D. has such a lack of stimulation and distraction that the subject may find it much easier to adopt an objective attitude toward even pain. His desire for stimulation and interruption in the monotony may work to his advantage.

In "forceful indoctrination" the use of physical violence appears unwise. To be sure, if the pain is sufficiently intense, it can cause a person to "confess" to anything, but confession is not the purpose of brainwashing, which attempts to change old ideas and implant new ones that the individual embraces as his own. A forced confession has no effect upon an individual's private, innermost beliefs; it is merely an example of a practical means of ending an undesirable situation. Also, in the face of force we tend to retaliate, a response that would certainly defeat the purpose of brainwashing, for retaliation would only help to maintain a clear definition of the "enemy" and hence sustain the prisoner's own beliefs.

It seems strange to have combined here the two subjects of physical pain and the acquisition of beliefs. Yet this appears to be the case not just in brainwashing but in many situations where we are unable to escape pain. We can alter that pain by our attitude toward it.

CHAPTER XIV

The Effect of S.D. upon Speed of Reaction

WE commonly find that as a result of certain experiences we feel dull, sluggish, and not very alert. In part, at least, we find boring experiences likely to produce such an effect. As S.D. is a monotonous experience, we came to question the effect it would have upon the alertness of our subjects. It would not be sufficient to ask our subjects if they felt more or less alert as a result of S.D., although they frequently volunteered the comment that it made them feel very dull.

We decided to measure our subjects' reaction time, which is simply the amount of time required to act after a given signal. For example, if one were trying to stop a car as quickly as possible upon seeing a red light, the reaction time would be the interval between noticing the red light and stepping on the brake. The reaction time of a trackman is the interval between hearing the starter's gun and leaving the starting line. Reaction time is meaningful only when the subject makes every effort to act as fast as possible, and, as we shall see, it can be influenced by many things.

We measured reaction time by a special apparatus designed for this purpose. The subject was seated before a panel that held a small red light; a switch was at his preferred hand. When the experimenter turned on the light, he automatically started an electric clock that measured to the 1/100 second. The subject was instructed to turn off the light as quickly as possible by operating his switch, thereby automatically stopping the clock. The time registered on the clock was the interval between the experimenter's turning on the light and the subject's turning it off. This particular test measured reaction time to a light stimulus. Obviously one can also respond to sound or touch, and there is a difference in reaction time according to the nature of the stimulus. For the average person the reaction time to light will be from 0.150 to 0.225 second, for sound it is 0.120 to 0.185 second, and for touch it is 0.115 to 0.190 second. The range for each kind of stimulus takes account of the changes in reaction time produced by changes in stimulus intensity. Generally the more intense stimuli produce faster reaction times.

Unlike many of our previous tests, practice does little to improve reaction time. At best, practice can improve reaction time only about 10 per cent. We eliminated this effect, however, by measuring reaction time until no additional improvement appeared.

We used fifteen subjects who were to be confined in S.D. for a total of ninety-six hours each, and they were tested before and after confinement. We did not use a comparison control group, as such was not necessary, for we already knew that no change between tests would occur in reaction time for control subjects.

At first glance it appeared that S.D. produced no effect upon reaction time. The average preconfinement reaction time was 0.174 second; postconfinement time was 0.175 second. Clearly these two measures were not appreciably different, so that we were tempted to state that S.D. had no effect upon reaction time; but such a conclusion would have been only half correct.

Of the fifteen subjects slated for ninety-six hours of S.D., eight called for early release. Thus we had a successful and an unsuccessful group of S.D. subjects, and when we viewed the reaction time data accordingly, our conclusion changed. For the successful group our conclusion stood, but for the unsuccessful group there was a significantly slower reaction time after S.D. Their postconfinement time averaged 0.200 second, which was statistically slower than their preconfinement measures. The successful group's postconfinement reaction time averaged 0.160 second. The apparent decrease is not statistically significant, but one can easily see how the two postconfinement measures combined to cancel each other and thereby give a spurious picture of the whole group.

These findings suggest that individual consideration must be given to those subjected to anything like S.D. Furthermore it seems essential that, where alertness and fast reactions are required, a screening test is in order. Such a test could be easily arranged by confinement in an S.D. chamber.

The data on reaction time are hard to explain other than by merely restating the empirical findings: For those who do not tolerate S.D. well there will likely result a significant loss in reaction time. We might suggest that S.D. has had a disruptive effect upon them and that slowed reaction time is merely one manifestation of that disruption.

The more exact nature of the changes in reaction time must be studied. For example, we should next measure it in relation to a variety of stimuli. We should also measure more demanding reaction time, or what is called disjunctive reaction time, in which the subject has one of two responses to make, depending upon the signal he receives. Clearly such research has more application to flight conditions than does the simple reaction time.

The subject of motivation is important to reaction time and should be investigated in relation to S.D. For example, if a person's oxygen supply is reduced, his reaction time will be increased. But if he *knows* that the oxygen supply is being reduced, he will maintain his reaction time or even improve it. In other words, he is able to compensate for a deleterious agent that he knows to be present. Alcohol reveals something of the same effect, in that immediately after a moderate dose of it, reaction time is faster, but this is soon followed by a period of slower reaction time. That an individual can compensate in the manner indicated is not so important in itself. It does illustrate, however, that very subtle factors can influence reaction times.

In as much as time of reaction may be vital in space flight, and since space flight may closely resemble S.D., it is necessary that such study continue. Our next investigations are to include the effects of S.D. upon disjunctive reaction time. We shall also attempt to determine what stimuli can be included during S.D. to erase the negative effects during confinement. It seems possible that highly complex reaction times may be disrupted by S.D. even for the individual who can tolerate confinement, and we may need to invent new and more complex tasks in order to assess better the effects of such isolation.

The application of this research, it might seem, is limited pretty much to something like space travel for the simple reason that conditions similar to those in S.D. are not frequently encountered. To be sure, reaction time is of vital importance in our daily lives, but in the normal course of things we do not often experience confinements like S.D. At this point I am inclined to predict that we have hit upon something important with our reaction time measures. We may have gotten an indication of something fairly basic about man and the effects of isolation-confinement upon him. It would be of interest to determine whether isolation is of any importance to man. For example, would two individuals confined in the same S.D. chamber show the same reaction time results? Rumor has it that the Russians are now studying the effects of dual occupancy in a confinement cell. The claim is that they are interested in the effects that such treatment will have upon co-operation between two subjects. Studies very similar to this have been going on for some time now on a larger scale in submarines. In that case the confinement does not contain the element of isolation in the sense that S.D. does, and yet clearly there is isolation from the rest of the world.

Whether reports of the Russian studies are true, we should move in the direction of separating isolation and confinement effects. For example, in the case of those who do not tolerate S.D. very well, would the mere presence of another individual be enough to offset the negative effects of S.D.? I am inclined to think so. Would communication between them greatly alter the situation? Would one request early release if the other did not? What would happen to the relationship between these two people? I would predict that leadership would emerge more rapidly than otherwise under such conditions.

Let us return to reaction time and S.D. by way of summary. It appears that S.D. slowed down simple reaction time for those who did not tolerate confinement well. This finding, we submit, may indicate that more complex reaction tasks could be disrupted for everyone by S.D. and hence must be the subject of future studies.

CHAPTER XV

Those Who Stayed Not

In many previous chapters there has been frequent mention of those subjects who demanded an early release from confinement. It will be recalled that before entering the confinement cubicle each subject was told that he could end the experiment at any time he so desired. He was told of the presence and use of the "panic button," which if activated would effect his release. I should point out that we used the term "panic button" only in the popular sense of the word. None of our subjects experienced true panic or even anything close to it.

We informed each subject that to distress him or to "break him down" was not the purpose of the study. There was, therefore, the means of release from S.D. in the event that it became unbearable. Each subject was further instructed that if he pushed the panic button his confinement would end and he would not be allowed to return to S.D. That part of the instruction was necessary to prevent the panic button from being used as a way of causing a break in the monotony. The subject was also told that his pay for confinement would stop when he came out of it.

In the beginning of our studies we were very apprehensive about the condition of those who would use the panic button. We naturally feared the worst and expected these subjects to emerge from S.D. in a state of high agitation or real panic. That worry proved groundless. With one exception, when our subjects asked for early release they always came out in a quiet, calm, and completely collected manner. Very often after they had been out of the S.D. chamber for a few minutes they asked permission to return and complete the experiment. As indicated, this was not allowed, but their willingness to return to confinement indicates that their needs for release were not serious. Roughly one third of those who demanded an early release belong in the above category. Another third indicated that they would be willing to return to confinement, but only at a later date, and a final third indicated that they would never return to it. But even those firmly opposed to it came out of it calmly.

The one subject who emerged in a disturbed manner left no doubt that he was very upset by S.D. Oddly enough, we were unable to find why he differed so much from others who pushed the panic button; he reported only that while in S.D. he experienced *fear* and that fear caused him to push the button. Beyond saying that he was afraid of losing control of himself he was unable to say what he feared. His first thought that he was losing control occurred after being in S.D. for about ten hours, when he suddenly and for no evident reason started sobbing. After this he resorted to prayer, and when that did not help he began to contemplate the panic button. He ended his confinement after eleven hours.

Every time I think of this person I think of George Orwell's book *1984* and its reference to Room 101. It was in Room 101 that political prisoners encountered their innermost secret fears. Our subject must have encountered in S.D. something like them. It seems that such fears must always be intangible, unknown emotions that have not been dulled by experience. Such was the fear expressed by our subject. He had only a nightmarish idea of his trouble, so that he was unable even to identify it. Obviously this is the worst kind of fear, as reason cannot be used to allay it. If his fear has been identified as, say, that of darkness or closeness, or something concrete, he could have at least partially dispelled it by a rational approach. But he was unable to do this because his was more in the nature of pure fear than a specific fear.

As I have already stated, the other subjects who demanded an early release from S.D. were not nearly so disturbed as the case above. Thus, in a way, their actions are less understandable than his. If they came out of S.D. in a calm manner, why did they find it necessary to come out? This, of course, was the question put to each subject. The answers they gave do not allow generalization, for the reasons were individual and must be considered one at a time. But first the general process of quitting S.D. must be described because it was very similar for all. Usually a person began to debate with himself about quitting. When he first encountered the idea of pushing the panic button, he was usually able to defeat it and talked himself into staying. The debate was a lengthy affair in all but one case, a subject who quit S.D. so quickly he did not have time for much of a debate; he walked into the chamber, and before we could get out and close the door he said, "I can't take this," and came out. All the rest of our panic subjects revealed much longer periods of indecision. After they first talked themselves into staying, they experienced great relief. It was as though they had won the battle, and at that point they felt able to complete confinement successfully. The relief was temporary, however, and soon the need to leave arose again. It was almost as if the difficult periods came in cycles. Once a person succeeded in getting past a particular period of difficulty, he was content, often even happy, until the next period. Few subjects were able to get past more than two of these difficult periods.

Apparently to fight off these recurring compulsions to quit required a great deal of effort, and by the time the third one came around they simply did not have enough energy to combat it. This was the general procedure experienced by those who quit S.D., but their reasons for being involved in such a course of action were very different.

Although monotony was ever present, almost none of those who quit S.D. gave it as the reason. It was as though they felt that a more legitimate excuse was necessary. Some subjects indicated that they considered it an admission of weakness to have yielded to monotony. Thus the reasons they gave for quitting may have been partially invented in order to provide a more fitting excuse for their actions.

One subject explained his demand for an early release as due to an obsessive idea. While in S.D. he got the idea that he had gone blind. Obviously while in S.D. he could not easily test his ability to see and so he had to come out in order to conduct such a test. He remained in S.D. slightly over two days. Most of the waking time of this period was spent in concern over his ability to see. He was not the only subject who thought about the sense of sight. Many subjects commented that for the first time they had a real appreciation of blindness. It is not suggested here that he deliberately invented a means to gain release. Undoubtedly he was not engaged in face-saving techniques; he was entirely convinced of the need to check his vision. His reasoning may sound implausible, but it is necessary to keep in mind that he had been over two days in S.D. Not only had he been without vision for a long time (probably the longest he had ever experienced), but he was also in a situation that was conducive to suggestion. I am sure that this subject, at best, had only a vague awareness of the meaning of his obsession. He was, I think, genuinely convinced that he may have gone blind and did not understand that this thought was merely a technique for getting out of an unpleasant situation.

Several subjects who did not push the panic button said that the thought of blindness occurred to them too. But before it became obsessive, however, they disproved it. They did so by pushing sharply against their eyes, and this quite naturally caused them to "see" flashes of light and they took these as proof that their eyes were still working. These people were very resourceful, and it is not surprising that none of them pushed the panic button.

One subject who did request an early release gave "severe headache" as his reason, claiming that the pain was so intense that medication became essential. We asked him to stay long enough for the postconfinement testing, and after about five minutes of it he suddenly discovered that his "headache" was gone. He had received no medication, he was still in the S.D. chamber, and yet his headache was gone. In all probability it was cured for the simple but obvious reason that its cause was removed, which in his case was the stress of S.D., and release from that stress eliminated the headache. Though this subject was the only person to quit S.D. because of what might be called sickness, there were two other subjects for whom S.D. produced illness. One was a person who always became sick at the stomach when he moved to a new location. He always had a period of vomiting when his family moved to a new home, or when he left home and moved to school, and while first in S.D. he had a bout of vomiting. He was undisturbed by his illness, for he had experienced it too many times before. He completed his confinement.

The other subject who experienced illness in S.D. had two attacks of asthma during confinement. He had a long history of a kind of chronic asthma for which no allergy has been discovered, and it is possible that his asthma was caused by emotional disturbances. (Some medical authorities hold that asthma can have an emotional basis, especially when no allergy can be discovered.) As he experienced asthma attacks in S.D., we may assume that its stresses produced the attacks, which were not severe, and he completed his tour of confinement.

If we can presume to suggest that the headache, the nausea, and the asthma were produced by S.D., we might then venture that S.D. may be a way to study some forms of psychosomatic illnesses. Admittedly we are on thin ice here, but the knowledge of psychosomatics is so limited as to warrant some guessing. If S.D. is capable of causing a response even mildly resembling a psychosomatic reaction, then here is a means of producing the phenomenon for study. But to return to the subjects who pushed the panic button.

Another subject requested early release from S.D. because of backache, a universal complaint of all subjects, for they simply lay on their backs too long before they realized the trouble. Almost all subjects found that they could end their discomfort by lying on their side with their knees drawn up in a prenatal position. This was the almost automatic discovery of all subjects save one. (We have found that it is possible to confine subjects on their backs for two days without any backache if special arrangements are made: if the subject is in an adjustable hospital-type bed, with the head and knees raised, little backache results.)

The subject who pushed the panic button because of backache had more than the stiffness and slight ache that accompany lying too long on the back. His was much more than the usual complaint. He had a series of intense muscle cramps in his back that were recurrent from an old injury. The cramps were so severe that he had great difficulty in moving or even reaching out for the panic button. His trouble had started when, as a prisoner of war in Japan, he had lifted some heavy cartons. In doing so he strained his back so severely that he had had trouble ever since, though reappearances of the cramps had always been produced by lifting. S.D. obviously neither required nor allowed lifting or anything similar. This was the first time his back muscles had more or less spontaneously reacted.

After S.D. he noticed the recurrence of a malady that he had not experienced since his prisoner-of-war days, when he had been plagued by boils. Fortunately this difficulty, as well as that of the back pains, responded to medical treatment shortly after his confinement.

Isolation in S.D. reawakened one other war experience for this person in an interesting fashion. Early in World War II he had been on the beach at Dunkirk. (Yes, he also survived Dunkirk!) While awaiting rescue, he, along with many others, was pinned down by heavy shelling. During that time he had an extremely vivid vision of his father, who said to him, "Don't worry, you will live to be an old gray-headed man." Memory of that vision was forcefully brought back to him on the day he was released from S.D. While in S.D. his beard had grown, and for the first time it had gotten long enough for him to discover that he had a gray beard. His hair had not turned gray, but his beard had.

Most of the difficulty this subject underwent in S.D. seems to have been recurrences of earlier troubles. Could it be that the stress produced by S.D. was enough to bring them back? It may be that these ailments during a prisoner-of-war period had served to produce special consideration for him and thus had somewhat relieved a bad situation. Could it be that the same technique was again used to relieve a bad situation that had some of the features of his earlier experience?

The reasons for quitting S.D. given by other subjects will seem less dramatic after the above account. However, we did not evaluate the reason before letting a man out; if he pushed the button, that was ample reason for release. One subject who was definitely on the side of a weak excuse claimed that he had to leave S.D. because he could no longer sleep. As with most people he had spent the first day of S.D. in slumber, and the prospect of confinement without this escape was too much for him.

Another subject ended his stay on the ground that he was underpaid. At first he had thought that twenty dollars a day sounded like a high pay rate, especially as no work was required. After he was in confinement for a while, he realized that he had been thinking of the usual eight-hour work day rather than a twenty-four-hour day. When he recalculated, he found that the pay was less than a dollar per hour, and he felt that the effort required to remain in S.D. was worth more. He also told us that he was convinced "that nothing more was going to happen." He was in confinement slightly over thirty-six hours when he pushed the panic button. He did not come to this easily, however; he had dismissed the idea several times. It seems that all of his attempts to adjust to S.D. turned out poorly. Calculating his pay rate occupied his time but produced a negative attitude to S.D. He tried to occupy himself by taking imaginary walks. At first this was a pleasant and successful diversion, but in every attempt he soon "got lost" and he was never able to complete "a walk," a condition he found mildly irritating. Negative and frustrating effects were produced until finally they became too much for him and he demanded early release.

In one case the presence of distractions did not prove to be of value. One subject found it necessary to quit S.D. because of his mental distractions. He started out in the usual manner by sleeping for the better part of the first day of confinement. Upon awakening he ate and noted that he felt good, perhaps too good, considering the conditions. He more or less "settled back" to see what S.D. was like and was pleased to discover that he could "smile at the darkness." He then dropped off for what he estimated was a short nap. When he awoke he was suddenly and persistently concerned with time. He became obsessed with the idea that he was losing all sense of time. By this he did not mean clock time; he meant the more general sensation of passing *through* time—from childhood to adulthood. His obsession led him to fear that he might somehow reverse the process and return to childhood. Apparently his childhood had been so difficult that he found even memories of it most undesirable. During confinement he had almost incessant and very vivid childhood memories. He stated that these were very unpleasant, but he would not tell what they were. The last one he recalled during S.D. he related, and, though it was not at all dramatic, it was disturbing enough to drive him out of confinement. As a child he had often awakened in the dead of night with a stomach-ache, and he remembered that these occurrences caused a great deal of anguish for him. In S.D., where it was perpetually the dead of night, he awoke with a mild stomach-ache that was accompanied by the kind of anguish that he had not known since childhood. When this happened he decided that it was time to leave S.D. Yet, like many others, he had difficulty in bringing himself to push the release button.

LENGTH OF CONFINEMENT

For those who demanded early release the average time of confinement was thirty-nine hours. For some this figure is not representative. There was one subject who remained in only four hours, another who quit after eleven hours. There was one subject, not included in the average given above, who quit the instant he reached the door going into the cubicle. It seems safe to conclude that if a subject gets past the forty-eighth hour he probably will not demand release; that is, he will not demand release prior to the stipulated lengths of confinement, up to ninety-six hours.

It also seems safe to assume that the average term of confinement for those demanding release would have been less than thirty-nine hours had not almost the entire first twenty-four hours been devoted to sleep. It was so often the case that when a subject could no longer sleep S.D. caused trouble. Thus it might be recommended that in confinement one should ration and distribute sleep so that it can protect one over a long period, rather than use it up on the first day.

As noted earlier, sleep was not the only protective device. Many subjects combated monotony by inventing mental exercises. Thus when sleep was no longer a method of escape, they reduced boredom by playing mathematical and word games. Reciting the multiplication table was one favored activity. Learning the alphabet backward was another frequently used activity. What is noteworthy is that without such devices S.D. was intolerable. Some people of fairly passive minds came to us, and S.D. controlled them. When the more or less automatic protection of sleep was no longer available to them, they were unable to cope with S.D. and had to demand release. It is highly probable that at that time in their confinement these people were very vulnerable. If they had not been able to gain release from confinement, there is no knowing what serious consequences may have resulted. To be sure, some might have mastered their difficulty and gone on to adjustment, but it is more likely that grave and negative effects would have resulted. In the more real situation of brainwashing it is at this period of vulnerability that propaganda probably would be very effective.

EFFECTS OF STRANGENESS

At one phase of our S.D. studies we were having trouble obtaining enough subjects. It was during the summer and, since Princeton does not have a summer school, few people were available. In an effort to find volunteers we sent an appeal to several colleges nearby. There were many responses to our advertising, but the venture was a failure, for nearly all of the people who came to serve as subjects were unable to endure S.D. Almost to a man they demanded an early release. Some of them had misunderstood the amount of time required for the work and so were unable to serve. Several thought that because our advertisement had stated twenty dollars per day as payment they would be detained only one day, though the ad had stated that they would be needed for *four continuous days*. But even those who understood what the work was like were not able to endure it.

There was such a uniform reaction from those who came from out of town that one wonders if factors other than S.D. came to operate upon them. Is it possible that being in a new environment doing a strange job produced an unendurable amount of strangeness? It would seem so despite the fact that what is outside the S.D. cubicle can hardly make any real difference to the man inside it. Why should the subject care *where* the cubicle is located? Does this suggest that the same cubicle and conditions located in, say, some other country, would have been even more intolerable? Clearly the answer is yes, for there pure hostility would exist outside the cell, but in our laboratory there was only strangeness to the subject.

It is my belief that these out-of-town subjects had one additional stress placed upon them. They knew little or nothing about the community in which the experiment was being conducted, but, more important, they did not know anything about the experimenters who were conducting the investigation. In the absence of knowledge perhaps they could have little confidence. They could easily distrust us, could easily find the situation disagreeable, and could easily imagine undesirable consequences to continued confinement. Their elements of doubt may have rendered S.D. considerably more intolerable. Whatever the explanation, it is nevertheless impressive that our out-of-towners so consistently wanted release. Altogether there were ten subjects, nine of whom pushed the panic button.

THE VIEWING BOX

In Chapter V we found that the use of a viewing box clearly separated those who stayed in S.D. from those who did not. It will be recalled that those who requested early release spent a great deal of time at the viewing box. We asked these subjects how often they had pushed the button to light the interior of the box. Most of them confessed that they had not kept an accurate account, but each automatically offered an estimate. In all cases they underestimated, and in some the errors were very large. One subject estimated that he had turned on the box light 5 times; actually he had done it 32 times. He was unable to explain his error, but we can be sure that it was not due to apparatus failure, for we checked that as a possible source of mistake. Another man estimated 25 times when the actual count was 121. Another said 12 when it was 23, another 14 when it was 31, and so on.

These estimates may be related to the nature of the material viewed in the box. It will be recalled that what the subject saw had little or no interest value; merely two spheres and a line or so. Perhaps the subject was unwilling to admit, even to himself, that he could come to spend so much time looking at so simple a thing. In addition, perhaps he was also ashamed that the task did not meet his needs and thereby keep him in S.D. longer.

There were two very unusual experiences of time confusion detected by use of the viewing box. One individual decided to "save" the viewing box until he was in his second day of S.D., or, rather, into what he estimated was the second day. Actually he started using the box sixteen minutes after entering the chamber. He revealed that immediately upon entering S.D. he went to sleep. When he awoke he felt that he had slept an entire day and was thus in the second twenty-four hours. His confusion was not restricted to time orientation; he was fairly mixed up about the entire experience though his confinement was considerably less than one day.

Another subject did just the reverse. He reported that he used the viewing box several times very shortly after going into S.D. Actually he did not push the button until almost twenty-two hours after he entered the cubicle. He too went to sleep almost immediately upon entering, and when he awoke he assumed that he had taken a short nap, and he then turned to operation of the viewer. Though his sleep had lasted nearly a full day, he estimated that it had been only "one half hour at the most."

We have all been confused about time lapse during sleep, but the extremes of these two subjects seem most unusual. It should also be noted that the subjects who did not ask for early releases never had time confusions of such magnitude.

MAXIMIZING THE WORST OF S.D.

Those who found S.D. so intolerable constitute a special group. They are people who have experienced a situation that has gotten to them in a significant way. This is not to say that S.D. has detected some fundamental weakness in their make-up, but it does indicate that they cannot handle isolation and confinement. Does this suggest that some people are more self-sufficient than others and that S.D. might provide a method of measuring it?

If it is correct to believe that, in some people at least, S.D. is a way of reaching some fairly fundamental constructs of personality, then it is natural to speculate about those features of S.D. that appear to be crucial. One can hardly resist wondering how the conditions could have been made more intolerable.

It has been noted that S.D. seemed to be worse for those who were not familiar with the general location of the S.D. chamber. Thus strangeness of environment may be a critical factor, the force of which could be increased almost indefinitely. Obviously I do not mean providing a *hostile* environment, for the rational beings would merely avoid and most certainly escape from it. Intended here is the causing of the same urge to escape without any external threat to the subject.

The strangeness of S.D. could be easily increased by introduction of some material from outside the cubicle. As it is now, the subject is left to himself, but more uncertainty in the situation could be arranged—for example, if the subject were allowed to communicate, in a limited manner, with the experimenter, only to have the communication break down. A mild annoyance and concern over the experimenter would be generated. In fact any change in the situation would probably be viewed with suspicion.

A change involving the experimenter would probably generate more than the usual attention, as most of the S.D. subjects revealed that they often thought of him. We have since told subjects that the experimenter is not in the laboratory next to the confinement chamber, that he is monitoring from a remote section of the building. This seemed to produce more of an isolation effect in the subject. When the experimenter was in the room adjacent to the chamber, our subjects often resented his freedom. In their eyes he had lights, books, a radio, freedom to move, etc. They, of course, did not expect anything else from him, but he was, in a sense, responsible for their confinement. As they automatically come to think about him, it would be easy to generate strangeness by changes regarding him.

Many subjects expressed the fear that they had been deserted while in confinement. They of course had no way of knowing that the experimenter maintained his vigil. The thought of being deserted did not disturb them except for the occasional person who wondered how he would be notified in the event of disaster or if the building caught fire. We had two people who became deeply concerned over the health of the experimenter. "What if he should suddenly die?" They were unaware, as were most subjects, that they could merely open the doors and walk out at any time they wished.

FINAL COMMENT

Actually the work in this area has only begun; there is a great deal more to do. To date many facts have been gathered, but very little theory has been generated. This work will in time contribute to the better understanding of man; at the present it has offered primarily just a promise.

Applications of this work have been attempted. I

have indicated the relation between S.D. and brainwashing. Others have pointed out the relation between S.D. and manned space flight as well as confinement to shelters made necessary by war. At present any use of S.D. data is an extrapolation. Many factors in the application of the findings are different from those of the laboratory, so one must generalize with caution, though until additional studies are made these generalizations will often be the only help available.

CHAPTER XVI

Diet and Loss of Weight

PROVIDING food and drink for our S.D. subjects was more of a problem than we expected. During the McGill University studies meals were simply brought into the cubicle. We considered this procedure to be too great an interruption of the conditions of deprivation. But we were handicapped because it was not easy to have refrigeration in the chamber. Any of the usual refrigerators produced enough noise and heat to be undesirable for our purposes. At first we solved this problem by providing sandwiches, fruit, and Thermos bottles of soup and water. This arrangement worked very well, as all these items would be easily consumed in darkness. Also there was no problem identifying the Thermos bottles, for those with smooth sides contained water and those with corrugated sides held soup.

All the food was prepared and placed in a food locker located at the foot of the bed within the cubicle, and each subject was told how to open and close it in the darkness. To this end a dry run was conducted prior to confinement. We felt it important that food odors be confined as much as possible to the chest to minimize their presence.

Each subject was informed in a very general way about his food. He was told that he would have soup and sandwiches, fruit and water, but he was not told the type of any of them. After release from S.D. the subjects were asked to identify what they had eaten; we were surprised to find that very few could do so correctly. The apples were always correctly identified, but the soup and sandwiches were another story. The types of sandwiches actually used were American cheese, boiled ham, and bologna, all on white bread. The soups were beef bouillon and tomato. The tomato soup caused little trouble, but very few subjects correctly identified the beef bouillon. Some thought that it was a special nutritional brew for the purposes of the experiment; some claimed that it was a watery broth they had never tasted before; others merely misidentified it by calling it onion soup, clam chowder, chicken soup, or vegetable soup. One subject insisted that both soup Thermos bottles contained tomato soup but that one was thinner than the other. It is hard to understand how these confusions could happen. It would seem that even if the taste of the soup failed to identify it the consistency would have prevented some of the answers given.

The identifications of the sandwiches were even more

confused except for the cheese sandwiches, which were usually correctly identified. One subject did call them peanut butter, however. The meat sandwiches were grossly misidentified by almost all subjects. Some identified all the meat sandwiches as being chicken salad, which, considering texture, was an almost ridiculous mistake. One subject said that, despite his dislike for tuna salad sandwiches, he had eaten all of them. Most subjects thought that they had eaten roast beef sandwiches, though some could go no further than to say "cold cuts." Several subjects invented a curious identification, claiming that they had had a combination of ham and cheese and even insisting that rye bread was used. Every now and then a subject said that whole-wheat bread had been used, that the extra nutritional value of the whole wheat made it desirable.

Some made correct identifications of the food and even told the amount, the number of each kind of sandwich they had consumed. However, the confidence in the identification was very weak even for those who were correct. Almost all of the subjects reported that they derived no pleasure from eating. All were very concerned about the food and water. They worried as to whether the supply was adequate, they were concerned over and puzzled by the lack of enjoyment of the food, and they usually contemplated some rationing system, especially for the water, but never carried it out.

S.D. EFFECTS UPON BODY WEIGHT

The stock of food available to the S.D. subject was more than abundant. In fact we deliberately overstocked the food chest because we expected overeating. We thought that, as eating would be one way to break up the monotony, it would be either prolonged or occur often or both. Thus we expected our confinees to gain weight. The surprising thing is that all but two *lost* weight! There was a great deal of individual variation, which was to be expected, but the length of confinement was not necessarily directly related to the loss of weight. For example, one man confined for two days lost seven pounds, but that does not mean that the rate of weight lost in S.D. is three and a half pounds per day. It is only in a very general way that we can say that the length of confinement is related to the amount of weight loss.

The table below provides the average total weight loss according to the length of confinement:

DAYS	POUNDS
1	2.7
2	1.8
3	3.0
4	3.7

The loss of weight by S.D. subjects is hard to explain. They eat the food and yet apparently do not receive full benefit from it. We calculated that the provisions allowed an average of over three thousand calories per day, and, considering their lack of activity, that amount should have yielded a slight gain. The two subjects who didn't lose weight were confined for forty-eight hours. One weighed the same upon release and the other had gained one half a pound. These exceptions are not significant and should be taken only to suggest the degree to which people can vary. It is of interest that on the average less weight was lost by those confined for forty-eight hours, perhaps because that length of confinement is a particularly difficult time. If people relieve tension by eating (and there are some who attribute the present-day overweight problem to that cause), then perhaps our forty-eight-hour subjects overate because of tension and thus lost less weight than others did.

Most subjects, upon being released from S.D., indicated that they were hungry, not of an empty stomach, but for specific foods that were their favorites, and particularly for a *hot* meal. Most of them remarked that never before had they realized how much the taste of food depends upon its being heated.

After we became aware that subjects lost weight, we wondered whether their strength was also failing. We tried to test this idea by measuring the strength of grips of our subjects, using a device called the "hand dynamometer," which registers in pounds the amount of squeeze one is capable of producing with one hand. As one continues its use, the strength of squeeze increases, and it became necessary to have a control group for purposes of comparison. We found that the control group improved their strength of squeeze by an average of four pounds, but that with S.D. subjects, upon release, the strength of squeeze depended upon the length of confinement: those confined for one day showed an increase in their squeeze of two pounds, those confined two days increased four pounds, and those confined three days *lost* three pounds. Thus we see that the strength of the person's grip follows the pattern of his weight. With short confinements, lasting one day, there is a weight loss and less gain in the strength of grip than should have occurred as indicated by the control group. With two days of confinement there is less weight loss and no impairment to the strength of grip. With three days of confinement the weight loss is larger and the loss in strength of grip is significant. This comparison does not intend to suggest that the loss of weight *causes* the loss of strength of grip. Such small weight losses could hardly be expected to so affect the strength of an individual. It merely happens that weight and strength behave in a similar manner when subjected to S.D.

A CHANGE OF FOOD

With one set of twenty subjects we changed the food provisions for several reasons. For one thing, they were wearing face masks (described in Chapter XI), which made sandwich eating somewhat difficult. We increased the calorie count in an attempt to offset the loss of weight. We still wanted that there be no sounds and that the subject lie as quietly as possible.

We abandoned the sandwich, soup, and fruit fare in favor of baby food put up in wide-mouth jars. It was possible to select a wide variety of foods, some of which were "main course" foods such as macaroni and cheese, spaghetti, and noodles and cheese. We also stocked many kinds of fruit such as applesauce, peaches, pears, and tutti frutti. All of the foods were pretested by the experimenters to determine their palatability when not heated. It was our opinion that these foods were of excellent flavor and that they did not suffer because they were not heated. We also provided small chocolate bars and water.

The confined subject was able to select a balanced meal by a coding of the food jars. Each jar had a plastic spoon taped to it. On the main-course jars the handle of the spoon was in the up position; on the fruit jars it was down. Each subject was allowed to select and eat as he wished. Most subjects ate a fairly balanced meal, but slightly favoring the fruits, which were considered to be refreshing. The supply was sufficient to allow a tremendous amount of overeating, but such did not occur.

The twenty subjects were to be confined for forty-eight hours. The average weight loss was 2.82 pounds.

Of the twenty subjects sixteen completed the forty-eight hours of confinement, and they averaged a loss of 3.43 pounds. The unsuccessful subjects averaged a loss of 0.37 pounds, a figure that is very misleading, as they were confined for very different lengths of time. One unsuccessful subject, confined for forty hours, lost three pounds, while another confined for only eleven and a half hours gained two pounds. The record for each individual is provided in the table below.

Food Consumption of Successful Subjects, 48 Hours of S.D.

Subject Number	Change in Weight, in Pounds	Amount of Consumed Food, in Ounces			
		Main Course	Fruit	Chocolate	Total
53	0.0	20.20	40.00	2.0	62.30
54	−5.0	36.50	12.60	4.0	53.10
55	−3.5	80.00	23.60	3.0	106.60
56	−3.0	71.30	27.40	2.0	100.70
57	−5.5	07.75	23.25	0.5	31.50
58	−3.0	07.75	54.25	0.0	62.00
59	−5.0	38.75	15.50	0.0	54.25
61	−3.0	54.25	00.00	7.0	61.25
62	−3.5	46.50	46.50	6.0	99.00
63	−4.0	15.50	31.00	4.0	50.50
64	−5.0	54.25	31.00	7.0	92.25
66	−3.0	85.25	77.50	4.5	167.25
67	+1.0	15.50	15.50	2.0	33.00
68	−4.0	31.00	54.25	8.0	93.25
70	−3.5	23.25	15.50	4.0	42.75
71	−5.0	07.75	46.50	5.0	59.25

Food Consumption of Unsuccessful Subjects

Subject Number	Change in Weight, in Pounds	Amount of Consumed Food, in Ounces				
		Main Course	Fruit	Chocolate	Total	Time in S.D.
52	+ .5	06.00		2.0	08.00	9
60	−3.0	23.25	23.25	5.0	51.50	40
65	+2.0	07.75	00.00	2.0	09.75	11½
69	−1.0	03.87	00.00	2.0	05.87	5

The data from the preceding table clearly indicate that subjects in S.D. can expect to lose weight. The surprising thing is that they do not *consume* enough food to prevent weight loss. If we figure that four ounces of food is roughly equivalent to a hundred calories, our subjects averaged slightly under nine hundred calories per day. Although this figure is low enough to produce a loss of weight, it is still surprising that so much weight is lost in such a short time.

The amount of food consumed was highly variable, much more so than the amount of weight loss. For example, note that Subject 66 consumed almost four times as much food as Subject 70, who lost only a half pound more than Subject 66. At first it is hard to reconcile the data for Subjects 57 and 67. Subject 57 consumed 31.50 ounces and lost 5.5 pounds, whereas Subject 67 consumed only 33.00 ounces and *gained* 1 pound instead of losing approximately 5 or so pounds. Some of this discrepancy can be accounted for as much as two quarts of water during S.D., which by the water consumption, as several subjects drank would roughly figure to be a little over 4 pounds. Subject 65 gained 2 pounds undoubtedly because of the amount of water he consumed. Statistically there is no correlation between the amount of food consumed and the weight loss.

In the future we will have to keep a record, not only of the consumed food, but also the amount of water and the weight of the elimination products.

At the present, however, it is still surprising that our subjects do not eat more when an abundance of palatable food is available. It would appear that as there is so little activity and hence so little need for food the appetite is accordingly regulated.

CHAPTER XVII

Facts Without a Theory

In any area of inquiry events proceed at an uneven pace. At one point in time, knowledge seems to race ahead at a great rate, only to bog down suddenly to a snail's pace. There is no simple accounting for the erratic growth of knowledge, and it is perhaps best to accept it as merely the way things are.

As knowledge is accumulating, however, other things also happen even when the process is slow or stagnant. There is the almost inevitable development of theories that attempt to explain the whys of the data. Men develop theories in an effort to account for empirical findings as a way of bringing divergent facts under a single system.

This is not the invariant direction or order of things. Very often the investigator has a theory (or a hunch) about his study and sets out to test it. But then as the information begins to accumulate from many investigators, the theories change and gradually take shape until they finally have survived many tests though perhaps never becoming a final theory.

Theories not only explain things to us, they also

tend to generate new tests of themselves. A theory is rarely so well established as to be automatically accepted by everyone. They almost always present a challenge, not just to the informed scientist, but to everyone, to think up ways of disproving the theory. This is not bad; it is as it should be, one of the things that lend high excitement to the science of any field. One does not present a theory with the idea that it will be accepted; instead he offers something he knows in advance will be challenged at every quarter. The overwhelming importance of that theory, however, is not whether it is correct but whether it stimulates new ideas, new investigations, more facts, more information, and finally a revised theory so that the unending process may begin again at a higher level of understanding. Perhaps the greatest of all mistakes is for man to assume that he understands, for, when he feels that he knows the why of any particular thing, he ceases all efforts to conduct further investigations. And of course we, at this point in time, know only the most superficial explanations for most things. Thus theories are the necessary agent to cause man to go beyond the obvious, past the shallow, below the superficial, in his quest for knowledge.

The reader may have wondered about the title of this chapter. How could I recognize the need for theory and at the same time work in an area conspicuous by its lack of theory? I have no ready answer for that except to say that we should consider the nature of the work concerning S.D. and what some people have said about it.

We might dismiss this whole problem by saying that this area is too young to have a theory. But that is not altogether the truth. I think that the lack of theorizing here is due to the nature of the various investigations. They have been conducted, it seems to me, in as eclectic a way as can be imagined. They have touched on a great variety of many aspects of human behavior and have not traveled very far in any one aspect. It is not that S.D. investigators have asked too many questions; it is rather that they have asked too great a variety of questions, so that we know a very little bit about a great number of different reactions to S.D. In a sense this is a testimony to the dramatic stimulation of such work. It fires the imagination of all who come into contact with it, and the product of these stimulated imaginations has naturally been many kinds of investigations. Thus to explain the whys of S.D. is almost to explain man himself. It may be that it does not warrant a theory all to itself, but that it should merely become a subsystem in any effort to explain human conduct. But again that looks like the easy way out. Furthermore who can resist speculating about the whys of S.D.? At practically every presentation of our findings we have certainly yielded to the irresistible urge to speculate, if not theorize, on explanations. If these diverse speculations were to be collected and molded into a neat, consistent statement, it perhaps could be dignified by the title of a theory. In a moment we will see a few such efforts made by some others.

Another problem hampering a theory of S.D. is what I would call the reverse view. Many people seem to ask what effect S.D. will have upon the personality of a subject. They seem to see it as a way of changing personality. I cannot imagine such to be the case. In the first place, the experience is not intense or long enough to produce deep-seated results. The more correct way to ask this question is the reverse; that is, how do different personalities react to S.D.? We should not view it as a dramatic test that disintegrates personality; instead we should look for the kinds of reactions that are associated with different personalities. This somewhat innocent-sounding statement is not a simple suggestion.

Another confusion that may have discouraged theoretical considerations of S.D. is its all too quick associations with brainwashing. Very suddenly man became aware of the Communists' ability to manipulate the "thinking" of their prisoners, an act seen as the violation of an individual's last defense, the invasion of his innermost privacy. This was a horror of unbelievable dimensions brought to his most sacred self. We were, and are, revolted by the idea that our thinking can be manipulated by others, that we can be *controlled* against our desires. The facts of brainwashing were the final indignity of man to man. It was only natural that S.D. should be compared with it, for they were similar in some ways and were very dramatic. Thus the theory of brainwashing was automatically, and incorrectly, applied to S.D.

There is little doubt that S.D. could lead to a better understanding of brainwashing, but it is unlikely that such study would help much in the problem of a theory of S.D. Such activity would be a worth-while *application* of S.D. work, but would not lend itself necessarily to theorizing—nor should it.

To this point I have given the impression that S.D. is devoid of theory, but such is not the case. In addition to what might be called the minor speculations of nearly every investigator, there have been several major attempts at theorizing that are worthy of consideration.

Dr. Donald B. Lindsley, a physiological psychologist at the University of California, has theorized about S.D. in neurological terms. He places a great deal of significance upon the brain-stem reticular formation (see our considerations of this brain mechanism in Chapter XIII on pain).

It will be remembered that the reticular formation monitors messages coming into and going out of the brain. Because of its strategic location it has been thought to exert a vast influence on many aspects of human behavior. It has been applied to the sleep-wakefulness problem, to attention, perception, and learning, to motivation and drive, etc., all of which attest to its importance, even though it may overextend its usefulness.

A very simple way to consider the reticular formation is to imagine that it is a way station for all messages going to and from the brain. It looks over the neural traffic, inhibits some messages and enhances others, as though it were exerting something of a selective function, the nature of which must in part depend upon the total amount and kinds of neural events occurring at any given time. Thus it is obvious that such conditions as S.D. will probably decrease the amount of neural activity passing through the reticular formation. If this is the case, then the "importance" of any given set of neural events may be greatly enhanced. Said more simply, under the conditions of S.D. the human may be able to content himself with ideas or cognitions that he would otherwise simply dismiss.

Professor Lindsley goes on to say that, if S.D. were carried out in the extreme, to reduce neural activity to an absolute minimum, "stimulus hunger" would be generated. And furthermore, that if such a condition were not generated (which after all would be a form of neural activity), the void that existed could lead only to boredom, inactivity, and ultimately sleep. It will be recalled that many S.D. subjects do sleep a great deal during confinement.

Another feature of Professor Lindsley's theory has

to do with what is called the *centrifugal afferent control* (C.A.C.) This system exerts a regulation over the sensory input system so that the human neural network resembles the automatic volume control (A.V.C.) found in radio. A.V.C. has the function of increasing weak signals and reducing surges so that an even volume level is maintained. The C.A.C., using the level of activity generated in the cortex and in the reticular formation, exerts the same kind of control over sensory input signals.

I have not given the full account of Dr. Lindsley's theory, nor is such necessary in order to see where we are headed. What he has done is to show the neurological mechanisms that will be affected by S.D. In this he has done a service, for he has brought S.D. to a physiological basis, which is, in my opinion, a sound position. I, for one, find it easy and exciting to theorize about the effects of S.D. according to his theory.

Professor J. S. Bruner, of the Department of Social Relations at Harvard University, has directed our efforts at theory to a different level. Actually he has concerned himself with a theory about the development of perception, but in it he considers the possible effects of S.D. He suggests that we perceive and deal with our environment by a set of models or expectancies that have been gradually acquired from birth. These are "strategies" for dealing with the normal world, such as the expectation of being burned when one touches the flame, based upon previous experience with flames.

Professor Bruner goes on to say that if the organism is sensorially deprived during early life it will never develop these strategies and will hence deal inadequately with the environment. Our strategies are not finished products; we constantly monitor them and change them as dictated by new experiences. Professor Bruner believes that S.D. disrupts the evaluation processes of our various strategies so that they *cannot* be corrected and changed. Thus S.D. can be viewed only as a disruptive influence. It causes a period of no progress in our never-ending process of strategy molding. It is not entirely clear whether the cognitive process would come to a standstill, because of S.D., or deteriorate. In either case, however, a testable hypothesis is possible.

It is easily possible to see merit in the theories of both Dr. Lindsley and Professor Bruner, but at the same time it is impossible not to speculate in a somewhat different direction. (And to call it "speculation" is much more accurate than to label it "theory.") This direction is what may be termed loosely as man's need for change. This is not offered as an original idea, for it isn't; indeed the idea is so universal as to have perhaps no originator we may give credit to.

I believe that the human cannot long endure a completely homogeneous situation no matter how good or desirable it is. What is homogeneous soon becomes boring and undesirable. Caviar and champagne may be very desirable for breakfast, but not for long as a steady diet. No matter how positive a thing may be, it loses its value under unvarying use. Man's appetites soon become jaded, so that he ever seeks new gratifications or, failing this, finds increasing complaint with his status quo.

If by his achievements man becomes bored with it all, even if that all is most desirable by ordinary standards, he will look for change even if he has to destroy his present circumstances; if he cannot build new and differently, in order to depart from the old, he will rid himself of it so that a change is effected.

Admittedly these are very broad statements and at best can express only a personal opinion. Nonetheless the role of man in sensory deprivation can easily conform to these notions. Never before has man had so little opportunity to change his circumstance. Never before has he become so totally dependent upon himself (and to discover how little that is can be a frightening experience). In S.D. the opportunity for variation or change resides only in one's mind. For some this is possible, though in most cases not an easy task. For most the reduction of opportunity and the dependence upon self create a difficult situation. Some escape, at least for a while, by sleeping, but that soon ceases to solve the problem of boredom. The simple case, then, is that man does not well endure the conditions of S.D. because it affords almost no variation of the few stimuli presented to him. That there are some stimuli is perhaps the only way that S.D. could be tolerated. And note what happens to the evaluation of those stimuli. They become very enjoyable and desirable. A simple white light to which man would not under usual circumstances give any consideration now becomes a thing of wonder and worthy of prolonged study and thought. Man's jaded sensory world takes on a new meaning as a result of S.D. The ordinary, the usual, the almost unnoticed of our everyday world become, under S.D., very desirable experiences, and perhaps for the first time we come to appreciate the value of our ever-changing stimulus world. And if it could mean that man would better utilize the information so constantly available to him, then one would recommend periodic sessions of S.D. for all.